# IMPERIAL LIFE IN
# THE QING DYNASTY

*Cover*

**EMPEROR QIAN LONG ON A HORSE**
Length: 192 cm
Width: 90 cm

Painted in Chinese ink and colour by an unnamed court painter, this painting shows Qian Long in a dragon robe on a horse. The Manchu people placed great importance on hunting as they saw it as a means to maintain the military prowess of their Bannermen.

*Editors*
Grace Wong
Goh Eck Kheng

*Book Design*
Goh Eck Kheng

*Photography*
Hong Tiong Peng

*Cartography and borders*
Lim Tiong Ghee

Published by
Historical and Cultural Exhibitions Pte Ltd
The Empress Place
Singapore 0617

Produced for Historical and Cultural Exhibitions Pte Ltd by
LANDMARK BOOKS PTE LTD
5001, Beach Road, 02-73/74, Singapore 0719

ISBN 981-00-0948-8 (trade paperback)
ISBN 981-00-0947-X (hardback)

Typeset by Superskill Graphics Pte Ltd
Colour Separation by Eray Scan Pte Ltd
Printed in Singapore by Khai Wah Litho Pte Ltd

*Exhibition Curator*
Tie Yuqing & Wang Yunying, Shenyang Palace Museum
Grace Wong, Historical and Cultural Exhibitions Pte Ltd

*Exhibition Design*
Staples & Charles, Ltd., Washington D.C.

*Lighting Design*
William Riegel, New York

# Imperial Life in the
# QING DYNASTY

Treasures from the
Shenyang Palace Museum, China

THE EMPRESS PLACE
CULTURE BY THE SINGAPORE RIVER

*(Overleaf)*

**LARGE DUO CAI
PORCELAIN DISH**
**Diameter: 50.5 cm**
**Height: 8.5 cm**

*Duo Cai is a style of decorating porcelain by underglazing and overglazing with patterns of contrasting colours. Popular during the Kang Xi, Yong Zheng and Qian Long periods, the favoured motifs were of flowers and birds. This example shows a pair of phoenixes meeting among intertwined branches within a ring of lotuses. This example is made rare and exceptional in that it is also decorated with the eight Buddhist treasures: jar, conch shell, umbrella, canopy, lotus, wheel of the law, fish and mystic knot.*

**YELLOW JADE CUP**
**Height: 10 cm**
**Diameter at mouth: 7.3 cm**

*The qualities of the rare and valuable yellow jade of Chinese origin is evident in this magnificent cup. The translucence of the vessel is highlighted by the eddies, swirls and animal faces delicately engraved on its surface.*

# Contents

# Foreword

**JADE SEAL WITH BOXES**
Height: 11.6 cm
Face: 12.5 x 12.5 cm

*This seal, made of jade of Chinese origin, was conferred on Emperor Shun Zhi (1638 — 1661), the first Qing ruler to reign from Beijing. Carved from a block of green jade, it has a compelling image of a dragon coiled protectively over a large pearl. The impression face of the seal is square and is inscribed with Manchu and Chinese characters.*

*Imperial Life in the Qing Dynasty: Treasures from the Shenyang Palace Museum of China, is the first in a series of exhibitions of Chinese relics to be held in Singapore under an agreement between Singapore and the People's Republic of China on economic co-operation in tourism.*

*This exhibition is housed in the newly restored Empress Place Building. The restoration of this neo-classical building reflects Singapore's commitment in preserving our historical heritage for future generations. The building promises to be a historical landmark, a notable tourist attraction, and also an ideal site for major exhibitions like the Qing dynasty relics.*

*These 312 treasures from China's last dynasty have never been exhibited outside China. I hope this show will generate interest in the artefacts themselves and in the history and preservation of the arts, and that visitors will be able to appreciate the artistic masterpieces of a bygone era.*

**B G Lee Hsien Loong**
Minister for Trade and Industry

# Preface

*t is the artistic and cultural life of a country which gives it its own unique identity and richness, the qualities so essential to a successful tourism industry.*

*Unfortunately, that direct relationship between tourism and the arts is not more widely recognised and accepted.*

*It is from this standpoint that we perceive the strong link between the cultural exhibitions staged at The Empress Place museum and our own tourism effort. More than that, we believe this series of exhibitions will play a major role in stimulating tourism for all parties involved.*

*So it is with particular pleasure that we welcome to The Empress Place, for its first exhibition, these treasures from The Shenyang Palace Museum of the People's Republic of China. We also take pleasure in welcoming the establishment of a tourism office, marketing China, which will operate in conjunction with the exhibition.*

**Lim Chin Beng**
Chairman
Singapore Tourist Promotion Board

# Introduction

Joseph Chew & Grace Wong

**BLUE-AND-WHITE
PORCELAIN DISH
DECORATED WITH RED-
OVERGLAZED
DRAGONS**
**Diameter: 48 cm**
**Height: 9 cm**

*This very fine porcelain dish of the Qian Long period was made at the imperial kiln in Jing-dezhen. Five dragons, overglazed in vivid red, chase a pearl amind the swirling cloud and wave motifs rendered in under-glazed blue.*

Imperial Life of the Qing Dynasty, an exhibition of over 300 artefacts and national treasures from The Shenyang Palace Museum, People's Republic of China, unfolds the hidden lifestyle of the Manchu emperors and their empresses.

For centuries, the 'Son of Heaven' who ruled the 'Central Kingdom' has never ceased to be a focal point of curiosity. Almost every detail of his life was shrouded in mystery and it was only in recent years, after the records of the Forbidden City were opened for public examination, that we have managed to gain a better understanding of imperial life.

To his subjects, the emperor lived a life of grandeur and lavishness that was totally alien to them. Much of his time was spent in ritual activity: at court, he sat regally at audience on the gilt imperial throne; he processed with an entourage of thousands in a pagentry known as Lu Bu; he offered homage at his ancestral tombs at Shenyang. For leisure, apart from the literary pursuits of painting and calligraphy, he liked hunting and used guns made in the West. Every three years, he would inspect the entire imperial troop in full ceremonial armour.

If the emperor was not on inspection tours, he lived in magnificent palaces surrounded by high walls and beautifully attired court maidens. He dined on at least 30 dishes in a normal every-day meal, and for banquets, the dishes would cover many tables set out in a great hall.

It is therefore a rare opportunity for us to reconstruct, in Singapore, some of the most important aspects of imperial life from the collection of the Shenyang Palace Museum.

On display are artefacts ranging from ceremonial items found in the emperor's throne room to the more ordinary objects of daily living. Beautiful garments and paraphernalia used during courtly processions, hunting weapons, military equipment and magnificent works of art all combine to form a rich tapestry of every aspect of Qing courtly life. Apart from this, a fully-furnished reconstruction of the Nine Room Pavilion once occupied by imperial consorts is also featured.

Each piece on display is a precious *objet d'art* connected with the Qing emperors, making the exhibition one rich in historical detail.

This is the first time these artefacts have been allowed to travel outside the People's Republic of China. Normally, they are housed in the Shenyang Palace Museum, one of the two most important depositories of imperial treasures in China. The collection can be traced to the reign of Emperor Qian Long (1711 — 1799) when, by edict, large quantities of artefacts made of gold, silver, jade, porcelain or cloisonne were transferred from Beijing to be stored at Shenyang.

Together with these shipments, valuable paintings and calligraphic works were also sent. By the end of the Qian Long period, the collection of important treasures housed at Shenyang Palace had already exceeded 100,000 items.

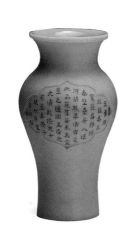

**YELLOW VASE WITH MANCHU AND CHINESE SCRIPT**
**Height: 19.5 cm**
**Diameter at mouth: 8.5 cm**

*This vessel, with the unusual colour of ripened corn, is made from a glass-like material which echos the quality of jade. This material was in fashion during the Qian Long period. The vase is unique in that it is inscribed with translations of a poem in Chinese and Manchurian.*

14

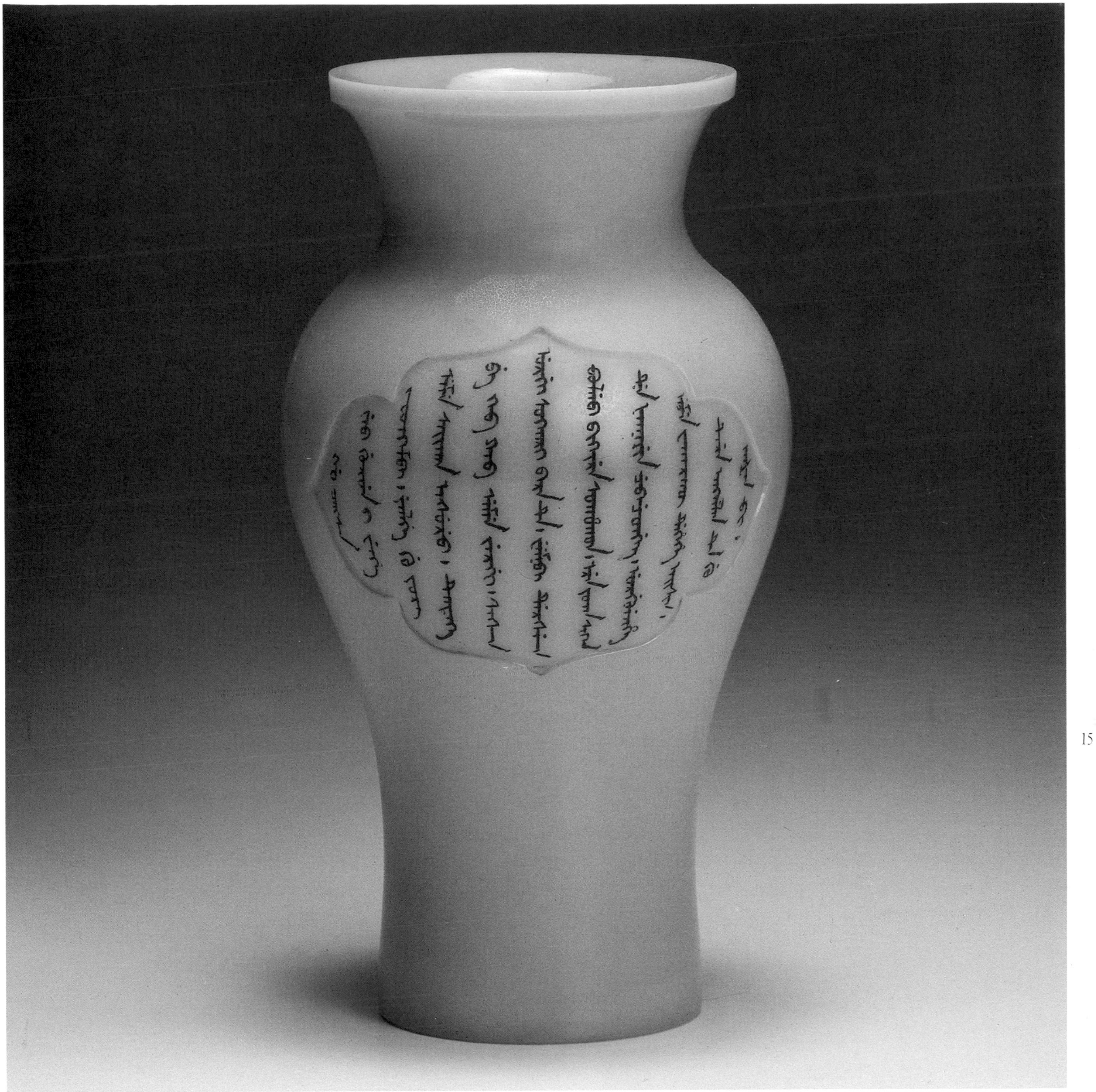

These treasures were moved to Shenyang partly for the emperors to bestow upon vassals and partly to meet the daily needs of the imperial court when they visited their homeland. Once, during the reign of Qian Long, over 100,000 pieces of banquet porcelain were sent to Shenyang.

Of greater historical importance are the collections of treasures directly relating to the ancient Chinese concept of kingship and state administration. These include the portraits of emperors and empresses, the jade seals bearing their titles and the jade tablets recording the important events of their reigns. Moreover, the imperial genealogical records, the histories of individual emperors, as well as the rare early history of the Manchus are also archived there. So too is the Complete Library of Chinese Books established by Qian Long. It comprises over 36,000 categories or 79,330

**RIDING GARMENT FOR THE EMPEROR**
Length: 113 cm
Skirt length: 112 cm
Sleeve length: 79 cm

*This is a woollen riding garment worn by the emperor when he went hunting. The front panel of the garment is cut shorter to facilitate easy movement on the horse.*

16

**SMALL GREEN JADE PANEL DECORATED WITH LANDSCAPE**
Height: 37 cm
Width: 26.25 cm

*Made of green jade of Chinese origin, this panel is decorated with a scene showing two scholars emerging from a grotto above a swirling river. The elder of the two gestures to point out a pine tree growing on the precipice.*

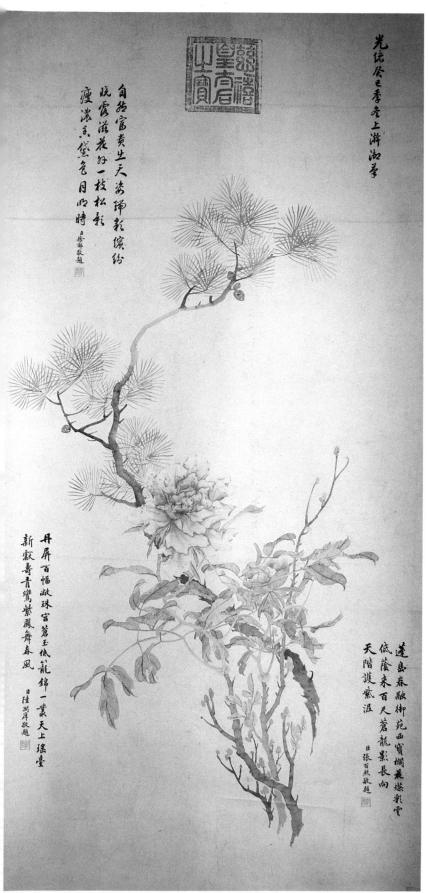

## PAINTING BY EMPRESS DOWAGER CI XI
**Length: 153 cm**
**Width: 75.5 cm**

*This painting was done in Chinese ink and colour by Empress Dowager Ci Xi who ruled China between 1861 and 1908.*

*This painting is of a peony intertwined with a pine tree. The flower is a symbol of material well-being while the pine represents longevity.*

*Drawn in the 'boneless' technique, this painting is a fine work of the school of court painting. According to literary tradition, the compliments on the painting were written by court officials on the order of the Empress Dowager.*

## SQUARE JADE INCENSE BURNER
**Height: 21 cm**
**Width: 16.8 cm**

*The stately form of this four-legged incense burner is taken from archaic bronze examples. A roaring lion, tensed and poised to pounce, is crouched on its lid while two dragon-like creatures wind themselves round the sides of the vessel to form a pair of ears. The incense burner is carved from green jade of Chinese origin.*

17

18

volumes compiled and copied by tens of thousands of scholars over a period of ten years.

For this exhibition in Singapore, a comprehensive collection of artefacts has been chosen to show not only the range, but also the very best of what is displayed at Shenyang.

This book illustrates the finest of these pieces and puts them within the context of the rich and opulent lifestyle of the glorious Qing dynasty.

Especially appropriate is the setting of this living history. *Imperial Life in the Qing Dynasty* is the inaugural exhibition of The Empress Place.

The building, with a distinguished history of 125 years, has stood as silent witness to the development and transformation of Singapore. Its role has been varied, ranging from housing the Legislative Assembly, to being the place for registering the birth of children.

Having undergone a conservation programme costing S$24.2 million, The Empress Place has become a museum of international standards. Firmly rooted in the past, it now plays a new and important role in preserving our heritage, and inculcating a sense of cultural awareness in all Singaporeans.

**BRONZE GOURD-SHAPED BOTTLE INLAID WITH SMALL JADE GOURDS**
**Largest Diameter: 33 cm**

*The gourd shape is a very common design element in Qing handicrafts. It was a popular symbol as the spreading of the gourd vine represented ever growing generations of descendants. This bottle is particularly interesting as it is a big gourd inlaid with many small gourds, truely symbolising an endless lineage.*

# A History of the Qing Dynasty

**PORTRAIT OF EMPEROR
SHUN ZHI**
**Length: 192 cm**
**Width: 68 cm**

*Shun Zhi (1638 — 1661) was the first Manchu ruler to reign from China. He was emperor for 18 years, but his reign was insignificant as he ascended to the throne at the age of six under the control of his uncle, Prince Regent Dorgon.*

The roots of the Qing dynasty may be traced to the woodlands north and north-east of China. There, from 1115 to 1234, Tungus tribesmen ruled the region under the dynastic title of Jin, and it was a descendant of these Tungus people that initiated the thrust that led to the unification of China under the Qing empire. This man's name was Nurhaci.

Nurhaci was a dynamic, young Tungus warrior of the Nuzhen tribe. Skilled in diplomacy and things military, he organized the Tungus people who had settled near Shenyang into feudal and military organisations called Banners. Each Banner, distinguished by the colour of its flag, was governed by Nuzhen aristocrats and leaders. They were to supply warriors for Nurhaci's military campaigns and to govern the civilian population.

The generals of the Banners were related by blood or marriage. Brothers, cousins, brothers-in-law, all supported by their groups of bannermen, formed a well-organised army which seemed invincible when faced with the crumbling Ming militia.

From 1609, Nurhaci began to make hostile advances at China, and bolstered by the region's natural wealth of furs, pearls, metal ore and ginseng, he proclaimed himself, in 1616, emperor of a new state called Later Jin.

In 1621, Nurhaci took Shenyang and

Liaoyang, and four years later, made Shenyang his capital. From then, his offensive began to bog down.

Nurhaci was wounded in an unsuccessful attack on the Chinese stronghold at Ningyuan in 1626 and, as a result, died later that year. He was succeeded by his eighth son, Huang Tai Ji.

Huang Tai Ji continued the route of conquest begun by his father. By 1642, he had taken the whole of Korea and Manchuria up to the strategic Chinese outpost of Shanhaiguan, the 'Pass between the Mountain and the Sea', at the eastern terminus of the Great Wall.

It is perhaps a paradox, but as much as the Nuzhen conquerers were bearing onto Chinese territory, the Chinese themselves were asserting their influence over their Manchurian aggressors.

As Huang Tai Ji pushed to overrun the Heilongjiang region, he began to take advice from defected Chinese generals and acquired weapons from deserters of the Ming army. Chinese literati were also enrolled as advisors to the imperial court. They brought with them the Ming administrative system and Chinese political theories. On their advice, Huang Tai Ji moved to balance the power among the generals of the Banners and sent his own administrators to manage the system, thus centralising power in his hands.

In 1635, Huang Tai Ji issued an edict changing the name 'Nuzhen' to 'Manchu'. The following year, he established the dynasty of the 'Great Qing'.

The full taste of victory, however, was not for Huang Tai Ji to savour. Having brought the Manchu forces to the threshold of capturing

**PORTRAIT OF EMPEROR HUANG TAI JI**
Length: 192 cm
Width: 68 cm

*Huang Tai Ji (1682 — 1643) was the eighth son of Nurhaci, the founder of the Manchu empire. History records that Huang Tai Ji was a soft spoken man who did not appear to take pleasure in being flattered. Neither was he perturbed by gossip. He has been recorded to have said, "I never listen to gossip. Right or wrong, I must see it with my own eyes before I pass judgement."*

22

Beijing in 1643, he died at the age of 52.

The push into Beijing and the final invasion of China was left to Dorgon, the half brother of Huang Tai Ji and the fourteenth son of Nurhaci. Dorgon, a strong candidate to succeed Huang Tai Ji, was thwarted in his ambition by objections from the other Banner princes. In a political compromise, he became Regent to his six year-old nephew, Shun Zhi.

Under Dorgon's leadership, the Manchus established Qing rule in Beijing and conquered north and central China. Any intentions he had in usurping the throne ended with his death in 1650.

Much of the Manchu success in China can be attributed to the strength of the Banner System and to the weaknesses of the Ming dynasty. During its waning years, the Ming emperors had defaulted power to corrupt and ignorant eunuchs. The military as well as the civil service were equally corrupt, and these, heightened by natural disasters and an impoverished peasantry, resulted in an open invitation for Manchu warriors to sweep across China.

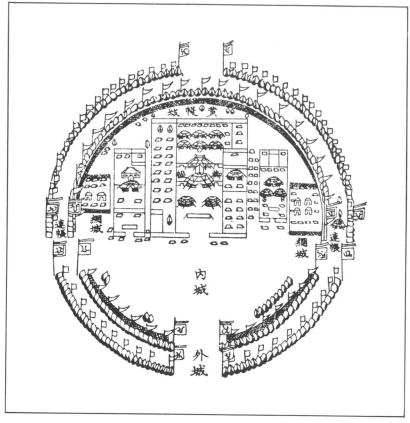

LAYOUT OF MANCHU
ENCAMPMENT

24

The Manchu conquest of China, from the capture of Beijing to the over-running of Taiwan, took 39 years. This was followed by a period of territorial expansion into west and southwest China, Tibet, Xinjiang, Mongolia, eastern Turkestan, Burma, Vietnam and briefly Nepal. This surpassed even the conquests of the Tang and Han periods.

It is not surprising that this era of rapid growth also marked the zenith of the Manchu empire. The early Qing emperors from Nurhaci to Qian Long were capable rulers. Industrious, disciplined and intelligent, they demonstrated their skills in administration and politics. With the exception of Qian Long, they were also very frugal.

Expenses were but a fraction of that of the Ming's. Control over budget was tight. Kang Xi

**LAYOUT OF MANCHU
ENCAMPMENT**

**MINE**
**Height: 12.5 cm**
**Diameter: 18 cm**

*Made of pottery and filled with gunpowder, these mines were placed on the ground and set off by a fuse. Mines of this type were used during the wars between the Manchu and Ming forces.*

ordered the department of works and each official to present a financial report every ten days. In his biography, he noted that the expenses for all the palaces throughout his 36-year reign was not even equivalent to that spent on one Ming palace in a year. Learning from the Ming downfall, he had also made drastic cuts on taxes paid by the peasantry.

In spite of all this, the Qing dynasty began a slow decline beginning from the later years of Qian Long.

Emperor Qian Long had a penchant for luxury, and his lavish spending on the arts shook the financial foundations laid by his father and grandfather.

At the same time, the strengths built into the administration by the early rulers began to show up as weaknesses in the ruling of a unified China.

The system of centralised government set up in

**CONCH SHELL MILITARY HORN**
Length: 27.2 cm

*Records of early military campaigns between the Manchu and Ming forces are full of references to conch shell horns. They were used in signalling advances and retreats.*

*However, during the Qing period, conch shell horns were mainly used in religious ceremonies. The sounding of these horns was such a common practice that an idiom evolved, describing people who talked nonsense as 'those who blew the conch shell'.*

25

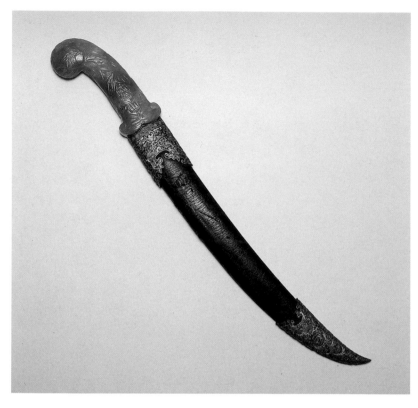

**KNIFE WITH JADE HANDLE**
**Blade and handle: 95 cm**

*This knife was Emperor Qian Long's personal weapon of self defence. In accordance to the ancient custom of giving names to fine knives or swords, this knife was inscribed with the characters which mean 'Rushing to Heaven', implying that the blade was so sharp that it could rend the sky.*

**KNIFE FROM MINORITY RACE OF SOUTH-WEST CHINA**
**Length: 47 cm**

*The leadership of the minority races in north-western and south-western China was an hereditary appointment from the Qing emperors. The leader of a south-western Chinese minority race carried this knife inlaid with coral, turquoise and other semi-precious stones.*

the early Qing period which allowed quick decision-making and confidentiality was ideal for an age of warfare and territorial expansion. However, the system was based on an extreme concentration of power in the hands of the emperor and his secretariat, resulting in a crippled civil administration system during peaceful times.

Furthermore, the Chinese system of civil service adopted by the Manchus did not have built-in checks and balances. Its efficiency and incorruptibility depended largely on the ability and alertness of the emperors. And while Kang Xi and Yong Zheng were particularly effective in this respect, often working up to 12 hours a day, the later emperors, being less hardworking, lost control of the bureaucracy and precipitated the decline of the empire.

**KNIFE WITH IVORY HANDLE**
Length: 47 cm

*This knife is a kurkri, a weapon typically used by the Gurkas of Nepal.*

The purging of Ming revolutionary elements in the literati when the Qing rulers consolidated power also contributed to the development of a handicapped civil service. In this, the emperor's hand was so heavy that capital punishment was not only meted out to individual Ming sympathisers, but also to his entire clan and all his associates. Often, a single line in a poem or essay, having been interpreted as a subtle revelation of rebellious thought, would result in the death of hundreds of able and innocent people.

Although this large-scale purge during the reigns of Kang Xi, Yong Zheng and Qian Long completely annihilated the remaining Ming supporters and succeeded in suppressing any anti-Manchu thought or feeling, it also produced a submissive and cowardly literati incapable of original thought. As such, there was no scientific invention during Qing rule and hardly any major scholastic achievement to speak of.

Even the 'great work' of the period — the compilation of a massive library comissioned by Qian Long — was counter-productive. The motive was to vet and edit thoughts and notions of anti-establishment from all published works. And to achieve this, the energies of the best scholars of the day were focussed on compiling, editing and copying thousands and thousands of volumes.

With an impotent bureaucracy and the lack of good leadership, the people of the Qing dynasty began to awake from the empty dream that China was the centre of the universe. Contact and confrontation with the West by the Manchus were followed by defeat. And defeat after defeat meant the paying of compensations, heavy debts, and the

**JADE TABLETS WITH BOXES**
Length: 28.6 cm
Width: 12.8 cm

*Jade tablets were traditionally used by emperors to record their speeches during the important ancient Chinese ritual of the Worship of Heaven. In the Qing dynasty, jade tablets, inscribed with essays outlining a deceased emperor's achievements, were also used when conferring the title of honour to the late sovereign.*

*This set of ten jade tablets, made from jade of Chinese origin, was completed in the first year of the reign of Qian Long (1736). It honours Emperor Shun Zhi (1638 — 1661). The front and backcover panels are shallowly engraved with the design of two dragons seizing a pearl, while the remaining tablets contain very fine and neat inscriptions in both Chinese and Manchu characters.*

opening of the first treaty ports.

With this, the import of foreign manufactured goods began to replace traditional Chinese handicraft. Western influence and the shift in public taste soon meant that the populous looked toward imports even in clothing and items of daily use. This inevitably led to the collapse of China's agrarian economy, and with general impoverishment and the carving of the Chinese pie, it was clear that the Manchus had lost their 'mandate' to rule. China was quickly reduced to a patchwork of 'semi-colonies' by Western powers. This situation built up to a strong demand for reformation, and when this failed to happen, the last hope for the dynasty was crushed.

At the centre of the turmoil, the strong-willed and misguided Empress Dowager Ci Xi continued to live the pipe dream of a past glory. Practising conservatism and being unable to turn the tide, she cocooned herself from the changing world and scraped the bottom of the imperial coffers to indulge in trifles.

By the 20th century, Qing China was financially, intellectually and morally bankrupt. In time, the tide of revolution became so strong that waves of insurgence followed one after another. In 1911, Pu Yi, the last emperor, was dethroned and a republic was formed, putting an end to the Qing dynasty and ten thousand years of imperial rule in China.

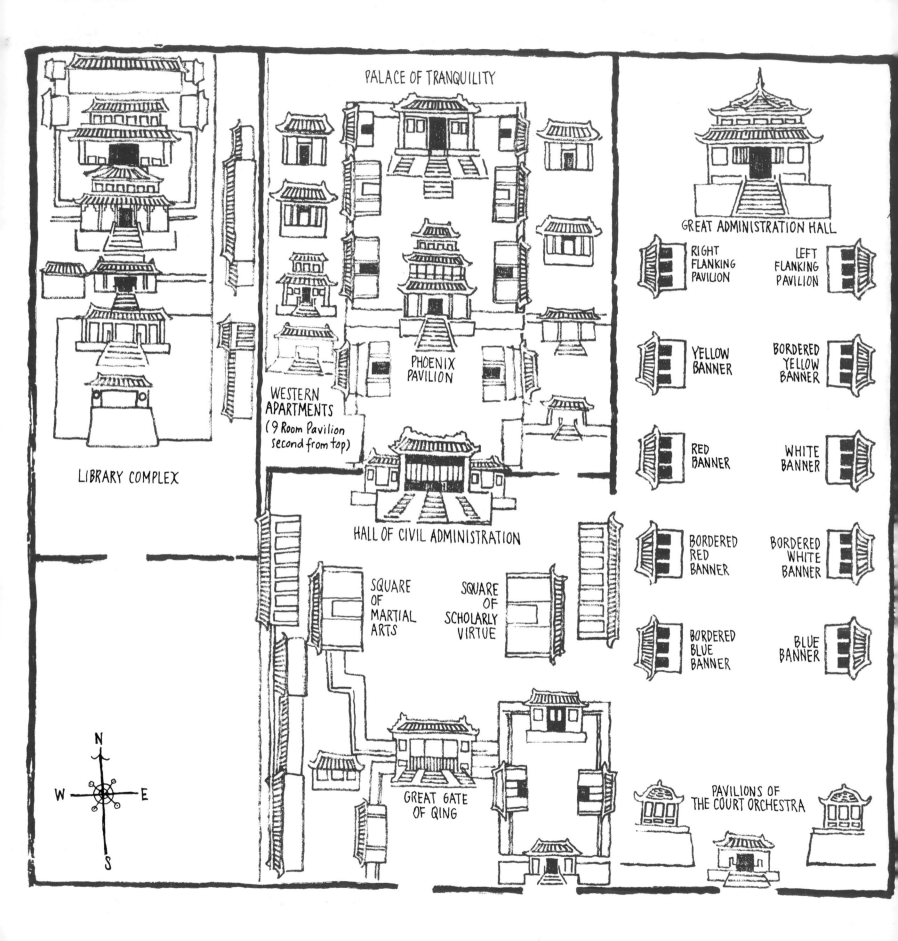

PALACE OF TRANQUILITY

LIBRARY COMPLEX

WESTERN APARTMENTS
(9 Room Pavilion second from top)

PHOENIX PAVILION

HALL OF CIVIL ADMINISTRATION

SQUARE OF MARTIAL ARTS

SQUARE OF SCHOLARLY VIRTUE

GREAT GATE OF QING

GREAT ADMINISTRATION HALL

RIGHT FLANKING PAVILION

LEFT FLANKING PAVILION

YELLOW BANNER

BORDERED YELLOW BANNER

RED BANNER

WHITE BANNER

BORDERED RED BANNER

BORDERED WHITE BANNER

BORDERED BLUE BANNER

BLUE BANNER

PAVILIONS OF THE COURT ORCHESTRA

N
W E
S

# Shenyang Palace

**MODERN MAP OF THE
SHENYANG PALACE
COMPLEX DRAWN IN AN
ARCHAIC STYLE**

Shenyang Palace was established before the Manchus ruled China under the title of Qing. Thus, it was to this palace that later Qing emperors, ruling from Beijing, returned when they visited their homeland for inspection tours and visits.

The Shenyang complex, apart from Beijing's Forbidden City, is the only completely preserved palace in China, and it has become an important museum.

The history of Shenyang Palace can be traced to the rise of the Qing dynasty. The Qings were Tungus who peopled the north-eastern region of China. In the declining years of the Ming dynasty, they were united under the leadership of Nurhaci and began asserting their military power on the weakening Ming frontiers, capturing, in turn, the strategic territories of Shenyang and Liaoyang in Manchuria.

When the Later Jin pushed east of the Liao river, Nurhaci established a capital city on a site north of Liaoyang, but in 1625, when he realised the strategic importance of Shenyang in terms of both logistics and communications, Nurhaci moved his capital southward to that city. Shenyang would remain the administrative hub and official residence of the dynasty for the next twenty years, right up to the time when the armies of the Later Jin surged over the Great Wall, ended the Ming

**THE OCTAGONAL
PALACE**

**DETAIL OF ROOF
DECORATIONS
SHOWING MYTHICAL
CREATURES**

era and established the Qing dynasty in Beijing.

Shenyang is a city with more than 7,000 years of history. The city was given its present name during the Yuan dynasty (1276 — 1368), and it was an important stronghold for the Yin kingdom as early as the Warring States (1122 — 221 B C). This role as a place of strategic importance was underlined in the Ming era when Shenyang was chosen as a centre of defence. The walled fortifications contructed for the Ming armies had gates set to the north, south, east and west according to established Chinese design. Inside, civic buildings, temples, shops and dwellings clung to the main thoroughfares laid in a cruciform grid. It was on this site that the Later Jins built their palace. And it is here that the history of Shenyang Palace begins.

Construction work on the Shenyang Palace complex began in 1625, and by 1632, the primary buildings had been completed. Following the grid established by the Ming fortifications, the Grand Administration Hall and the Pavilion of the Ten Kings — being fine examples of the traditional architecture of the time — are found in the east of the north-south axis. Built by Nurhaci, the Administration Hall was where audiences and imperial ceremonies were held. The octagonal building, with its heavy eaves and conical roof, was, because of its shape, also dubbed 'The Octagonal Palace' or 'The Eight-sided Pavilion'.

Sitting on an imposing 1.5 metre-high foundation, the building is lavishly decorated with wooden fan doors, overhanging eaves, ornate brackets, yellow glazed roof-tiles, decorative lintels and a pair of carved and gilt dragons set around imposing columns at the entrance. Inside, the

**VIEW OF THE PHOENIX PAVILION FROM THE SOUTH**

the building in which the Later Jins conducted their daily business of court. Built in the five-mountain style (two pavilions on each side of the main hall) and flanked by twin courtyards with corridors in the front and back, it is lined with richly carved stone balustrades and statues of auspicious creatures. The rooftop is embellished with coloured glazed tiles and inside, the beams carry frescos of clouds, celestial peaches and the like. This is the Hall of Civil Administration.

The living quarters of the emperor and empress lie on the elevated ground behind this building. The approach is by the three-storeyed

'Phoenix Pavilion' where, on its upper storeys, the emperor and his consort rested, read and entertained. This pavilion is the highest point of the palace complex, and the view from the top is unsurpassed. Here, the royals assembled to watch the rising sun and the vista presented is considered one of the eight finest views of Shenyang Palace.

The Phoenix Pavilion opens into a complex of five palace buildings occupied by the consorts of Emperor Huang Tai Ji. The central palace, known as 'The Palace of Tranquility', housed the emperor's private chambers and was also the venue when Manchu Shamanic rites were performed in Shenyang Palace.

The Palace of Tranquility has distinct Manchurian architectural features. The building has a large open plan room which is five 'chambers' wide and its entrance through the second chamber, leads to the imperial bedroom on the eastern end. The four other chambers contain altars dedicated to ancestors of the royal household. Here, an important Manchu shaman ritual involving the slaughtering of pigs and the cooking of pork is performed. A butchering table and large cooking pans are appointed in the room for the purpose.

The eastern, western and southern sides of the room have linked platforms, heated by burning coal and wood, called 'kang'. An altar rests on the western kang while the remaining kang are used as seats and beds. Outside, to the west and behind the building, a chimney rises from the ground to ventilate the kang, while on the southeast, there stands a ritual totem. Broken rice and pig's offal were placed on top of the pole to feed birds and, in particular, crows. This practice is traced to a

**COOKING PANS AND BUTCHERING TABLE IN THE PALACE OF TRANQUILITY**

**PLAQUE AT SHENYANG PALACE**

*This plaque commemorates the fact that the ancestors of the Manchus hailed from the East.*

37

legend that an ancestor of the Manchus was once saved from his pursuers by a flock of crows which alighted on him, making him appear from a distance like a withered tree. The totem thus commemorated and expressed the gratitude of the Manchu people to the birds for their help.

Four smaller palace buildings rise in pairs on either side of The Palace of Tranquility. These are the pavilions of four imperial consorts, and one of them, named 'Palace of Eternal Prosperity', was the birthplace of Emperor Shun Zhi.

In 1644, in the first year of Shun Zhi's reign, the capital of the Qing dynasty was moved to Beijing, and Shenyang Palace was relegated to a secondary status. The royal household no longer lived there, but the complex continued to be maintained for imperial use.

From the reign of Kang Xi, when Qing rule in China had been securely laid, the emperors began to make pilgrimages to their ancestral tombs around Shenyang. Thus, Shenyang Palace, now renamed 'The Convoy Palace' became once again a royal residence.

In 1743, during his first pilgrimage to the royal mausoleum as emperor, Qian Long, on visiting Shenyang Palace, ordered that new palace buildings be built for the accomodation and comfort of the touring royal family.

Between 1746 and 1748, two palace complexes were constructed to the east and west of the Palace of Tranquility. The three mansions on the east, known collectively as 'The Eastern Apartments', were the accommodations for the queen mothers of Qian Long and Dao Guang when they visited Shenyang. The 'Western Apartments', with their

**ANCESTRAL ALTAR IN THE PALACE OF TRANQUILITY**

**IMPERIAL SEAT IN THE PALACE OF TRANQUIL-ITY**

*This rest area, raised on a heated platform, was where Emperor Huang Tai Ji (1592 — 1643) died.*

**THE PALACE OF TRANQUILITY WITH RITUAL TOTEM IN THE FOREGROUND**

**INTERIOR OF A MANSION IN THE WESTERN APARTMENTS**

39

administrative hall, reading room and imperial bedroom were, on the other hand, reserved for the exclusive use of the emperor.

In the history of the palace, emperors Qian Long, Jia Qing (1796 — 1820) and Dao Guang (1821 — 1850) only occupied these buildings a total of six times. The imperial consorts who accompanied the emperors on their tours were, on their part, housed in an annex — the Nine Room Pavilion — amidst these palace buildings. The complex, unlike those constructed before the Qing conquest of China, do not possess strong Manchurian features. Only the use of yellow glazed tiles on the roof and green pelmets at the borders retain the flavour of the original palaces.

Yet another new development at this time was the addition of six warehouses to the complex. They were to store the vast collection of artefacts sent to Shenyang from Beijing by Qian Long.

In the thirty-seventh year of Qian Long's reign (1772), the emperor decreed that libraries, contain-

**DETAIL OF ROOF AND LINTEL OF THE LIBRARY COMPLEX**

*Unlike the yellow roofing of earlier buildings at Shenyang Palace, the Library Complex has black roof tiles. The green and blue wave motif on the lintel, representing water, is included in the belief that it would prevent fires.*

40

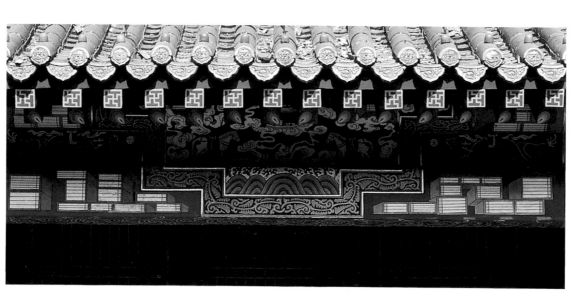

ing books collected from throughout the country, should be established. One of these collections was to be housed at Shenyang. It was also decreed that these libraries were to be built in the style of a famed Ming dynasty library in Zheqiang province. Thus, in the space of two years from 1781, a library complex centering on the Pavilion of Literary Sources, was built on the western side of The Palace of Tranquility.

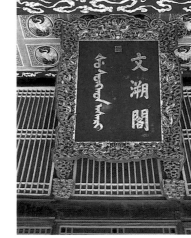

From the exterior, the literary pavilion appears to be two storeys high, but it has, in fact, three floors. There is a staircase on the western end, and the building is altogether six chambers wide. The roof of the pavilion is covered with black glazed tiles while the lintels on the front and back verandahs are dominantly blue and green, giving the library an elegance unlike that of the surrounding palace buildings.

To commemorate the completion of the library, a stone plaque bearing the calligraphy of Emperor Qian Long was erected in a gazebo set east of the main library building. To the south is a theatre comprising a stage and a makeup room. These faced the pavilion and bleachers from which the emperor and his courtiers could enjoy opera. Opera had become a favourite pastime of the court since the reign of Jia Qing (1796 — 1820). Behind the library are several more buildings intended to be used by the emperor for relaxation and the practice of literary pursuits.

With the completion of the literary pavilion, the entire layout of Shenyang Palace could now be divided into not only east, west and central sectors, but also according to the architectural styles and finishings of the different Manchu eras.

**THE PALACE TEMPLE**

41

collection of artefacts found in the palace. This news was greatly welcomed by citizens and foreigners alike, but the Qing government was already at its twilight and the dynasty was overthrown before it could even give a thought about establishing a museum of any sort.

In the early years of the Chinese Republic, Shenyang Palace was designated 'royal property' and maintained by the existing imperial administration. However, by the end of 1926, the local provincial government renamed Shenyang Palace the 'Manchurian Museum', with the purpose of implementing a scheme of social education and the promotion of culture and regional arts. This museum was inaugurated on 16th November 1927.

From the time of its opening to the present, the museum has had several changes of name and administration, but with each change, it has undergone significant development. From what was initially a museum of seven exhibition areas in 1927, it was expanded to eleven halls in 1932. Major restoration work was carried out after the foundation of the Peoples' Republic, and in 1961, the museum was designated a national treasure. Between 1985 and 1986, as part of the museum's 60th anniversary celebrations, many buildings in the complex were open to the public for the very first time. These included the library complex, the consort's Nine Room Pavilion, the palace temple, and the emperor's apartments.

From an enclave of royalty, the palace at Shenyang is now a place for the people. A monument of history and culture, it has the distinction of being one of the first, and finest museums established in modern China.

**ENTRANCE TO THE HALL OF CIVIL ADMINISTRATION**

# Pageantry and Ceremony

**T**hink of royalty and the mind paints a picture of throne rooms, pageantry and ceremony. Think of Qing imperial power and that image transforms itself into dragons, brocade silks, and courtly rituals many centuries old.

*Long*, commonly translated as 'dragon', is the king of all creatures and hence the symbol of imperial power. The throne and its accompanying screen at Shenyang Palace are covered with dragons.

The throne itself is known as the Dragon Throne, while the screen is intricately carved with 103 spendid dragons, posturing spiritedly. No two are alike, some stride among swirls of cloud and waves or fly in chase of pearls. Others are intertwined, contemplating the heavens.

The throne and screen were made about the time when Nurhaci established his capital at Shenyang and commissioned the Grand Administration Hall. From then, all important ceremonies of state were performed at that venue. For instance, the entire court paraded on the square infront of the Hall during the first Lunar New Year's Day after Huang Tai Ji succeeded the throne. Ministers, generals and officers assembled before the Grand Hall at dawn, and amidst the fluttering flags of the Eight Banners, they performed the Ritual of Homage, marching three

## IMPERIAL THRONE

*This intricately carved gilt and lacquered throne, and the accompanying seven-panelled screen resembles the dragon throne and screen found in the Hall of Supreme Harmony in the Forbidden Palace, Beijing.*

*Flanking the Shenyang throne are a pair of blue cloisonne elephants, each carrying a bottle on their backs. These animals were put beside the throne to symbolise universal peace. When the emperor gave audience, a white jade Ru Yi — the septre of authority and a symbol of good luck, and a carved red lacquer spitton would be placed on the throne. Crane-shaped candlesticks and incense burners in the form of pagodas and a mythical creature, would also be placed in front of the throne.*

46

steps, then kneeling and making nine obeisances to the emperor with their heads touching the ground.

A similar pageant was held there in 1644 when the third emperor of the Qing, the six year-old Shun Zhi, issued the edict for Dorgan, his uncle and Prince Regent, to cross the Great Wall, conquer Beijing, and establish Qing rule in China.

When the capital of the Qing dynasty was moved to Beijing, the civil and military officers remaining at Shenyang continued the tradition of performing the Ritual of Homage to the emperor at the Grand Administration Hall on the fifth day of each month. Homage was also made on the three major celebrations of the year: New Year's Day, the Winter Solstice and the Emperor's birthday. This was done even when the emperor was not physically present.

On these ocassions, the Bannermen and ministers filled the parade ground. Facing the Grand Hall, they took their places: yellow bordered with red, white, white bordered with red and blue

Banners to the east; yellow, red, red bordered with white and blue bordered with red on the west. The body of ministers filed according to rank while the Han Chinese officials took their positions south of the Bannermen whose colours were blue bordered with red.

These solemn pageants which accompanied the emperors of ancient China at court or during a parade is known as Lu Bu.

The ceremonies began during the Qin dynasty, flowered in the Han period, found development in the Tang era and was clearly established as tradition by the Ming and Qing dynasties. Lu Bu was originally a formation of soldiers which guarded the emperor, but with time, the function became a purely ceremonial one.

The name itself — Lu Bu — literally means 'Book of Shields', alluding to the book which recorded the order of appearance of the emperor's shield bearers when they formed the royal guard.

Under the court practices of the Qing, there were four versions of Lu Bu. The full and formal form was carried out during important state occasions such as coronations, royal marriages, New Year celebrations and the reception of ambassadors. There were variations used in the processions of court, another used when the emperor moved from place to place within the palace, and yet another form that was followed in military inspections and parades. The different forms were based entirely on the range of accoutrements used.

The full ceremonial Lu Bu was a spectacle. Preceeded by a cavalcade of elephants and horses and 16 trumpeters, an army of guardsmen paraded with over 100 flags and pennants. These showed

**CEREMONIAL CART**
Length: 4 m
Width: 1·25 m
Height: 2.11 m

*This ceremonial cart is made of rosewood and it was designed to be pulled by six horses. The wheels were placed at the rear of the compartment to make a smoother ride for the emperor. The cart was once used by Emperor Huang Tai Ji (1592 — 1643).*

**CEREMONIAL ARMOUR
FOR THE EMPEROR**
**Bodice: 76 cm**
**Skirt : 72 cm**
**Sleeve length: 37 cm**

49

*Every three years, Qing
emperors inspected their
armies to assess the military might of the dynasty.
This suit of ceremonial
armour used for such an
occasion, was worn by
Qian Long during the
early years of his reign.
The armour, heavily
padded and covered with
gilt metal plates bordered
by brocade, is designed
for actual warfare.*

motifs symbolic of strength and control: the sun, the moon, the constellations; the forces of nature such as cloud, rain, wind and thunder; and mythical animals including the white tiger, blue dragons and heavenly horses. Hundreds of other guards carried buntings, fans and umbrellas. Soldiers, fully equipped with weapons also trooped their colours.

There would also be a 173 piece orchestra, complete with sets of bells, drums, gongs and wind instruments. Most of the instruments, such as the bronze bells and stone chimes, can be traced to the

Bronze Age. Due to the deep-rooted Chinese respect for antiquity and tradition, antique musical instruments were seen as symbols of royalty and power. Thus, the choice of musical instruments for the Lu Bu was not only to set the tone of the occasion, but also to impress on the populous that the Qings had the Mandate of Heaven to rule China.

Apart from this large turnout, a retinue of attendants bore in procession an incense burner, a water jar, a sedan chair, a carriage and other paraphernalia — all for the comfort of the emperor during the event.

As a static display, the trappings of the Lu Bu would fan out from the door of the Grand Hall to cover an entire courtyard of several thousand square metres.

A Lu Bu procession was an expensive affair involving almost 1,000 people. In 1894, during the Empress Dowager's 60th birthday procession from the Summer Palace to the Imperial Palace, not just 1,000, but 3,787 people were employed in the parade. It was recorded that nearly 150,000 taels of silver was spent in the making of ceremonial garments alone. At that time, rice cost 1 tael of silver per Chinese stone (approx. 160 kg), and assuming that one man consumed 2 stones of rice over 12 months, 150,000 taels of silver would have been able to provide rice for 75,000 people for a whole year.

Such extravagance could only be within the premise of royalty and today, it is in the perspective of historical and cultural relics that we view this tradition.

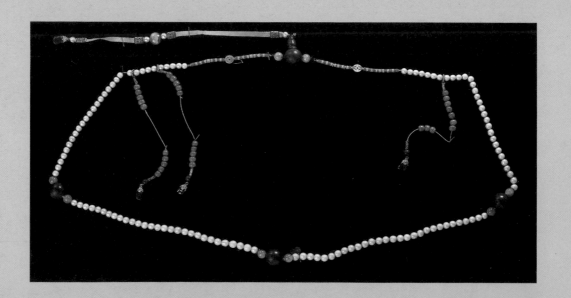

## YELLOW DRAGON ROBE FOR EMPEROR

Length: 132 cm
Skirt width: 107 cm
Sleeve length: 97 cm

*The dragon robe was the official garment of the emperor. The bright yellow fabric of this garment is made of satin-weave silk. Rich with embroidery, the robe features nine dragons embroidered in gold thread, water motifs at the hem and the twelve insignias of the reigning emperor and his house.*

*These ancient symbols comprise sun, moon, constellation, mountain, a pair of small dragons, some grain and flour, a pheasant, a waterweed, square or circle of flames, ceremonial vessels, an axe and an auspicious design.*

*Although imperial dragon robes are mostly yellow, the emperor wore different coloured robes for different ceremonies. When he sacrificed to the god of grain and when praying for rain, he wore blue. He wore red when he prayed at the Altar of the Sun during the spring equinox, and white was the colour he would wear when he worshipped at the Altar of the Moon.*

## EMBROIDERED DARK BLUE BROCADE OUTER COAT

Length: 113 cm
Sleeve length: 74.5 cm

*For important ceremonies such as the Spring Planting Ceremony, the presentation of colours to a general in a military campaign, victory ceremonies, birthday celebrations and when a princess married, the emperor would don the only dark blue garment he would ever wear. This outer garment, worn over the dragon robe, is the Jun Fu.*

*The Jun Fu is made of brocade and embroidered with four dragon medallions on the front, back and shoulders. As the Jun Fu was originally worn at the rituals performed during the Worship of Heaven, only nine of the twelve royal insignias were embroidered on the garment to express the emperor's humility before the gods.*

## MINK OVER-GARMENT

Length: 100 cm
Skirt width: 86 cm
Sleeve length: 63 cm

*Fur garments were an essential and practical part of official court apparel because of the bitter cold of Manchurian winters. However, only the emperor, his immediate family and favoured officials were allowed to wear mink, which was already considered very precious in the 16th century. Mink was one of the three treasures of Manchuria, the others being ginseng and Wu La grass, a common grass which the poor used as insulation against the severe cold of winter.*

## CEREMONIAL PEARL NECKLACE

*Made of 108 Eastern pearls, this ceremonial pearl necklace is worn over the Jun Fu, the outer garment for a dragon robe. Eastern pearls, found in the north-eastern Songhua river basin, are known for their large size and lustre. They were recognised as items of great value during the early Qing period.*

*This necklace has four short strands of coral beads attached at intervals to the pearls. It is worn with the longest strand of coral down the back and the shorter three strands in the front.*

## YELLOW 'KESI' DRAGON ROBE FOR EMPRESS

Length: 137 cm
Skirt : 103 cm

*This bright yellow garment decorated with eight dragon medallions was worn by the empress during ceremonial occasions. While many dragon robes have their designs embroidered onto the garment, the patterns on this robe was done on the cloth in tapestry weave. Called 'Kesi', the technique involved covering the undyed warp (longitudinal threads in the weave) with a design produced by the polychrome weft (horizonal threads).*

53

# The Pavilion of Continuing Thought

**CORAL AND JADE
HAIRPINS WITH PEARLS**
Width of ornament: 7.5 cm
Length: 6.25 cm

*This pair of ladies' hairpins is made of red coral, natural pearls and emerald green jadeite from Burma. The materials are cleverly used for different effects: the rosy petals of the peony, the lush green of its leaves, the sparkling dew drops on the flower, and the colourful butterfly resting atop the blossom.*

The Nine Room Pavilion or The Pavilion of Continuing Thought is a unique building in the Shenyang Palace complex. Commissioned in 1746 by Emperor Qian Long, and taking two years to complete, the pavilion, with its serene setting, was where the consorts who accompanied the emperor to Shenyang lived.

The Qing emperors had many empresses and consorts. Nurhaci had 14 official consorts whilst Huang Tai Ji had 5. After they established rule in China, it was decided that the Qing emperors should follow the Ming practise of having one empress and nine consorts of various ranks.

However, Emperor Kang Xi in his lifetime had 25 consorts and another 29 ladies of title — far exceeding the quota. Qian Long was not to be deprived. He had 24 consorts and 16 noble ladies. The later emperors were not so lucky. Both Emperor Tung Zhi and Guang Xu had just one empress each and three and two consorts respectively. From this, it is clear that the emperors did not bring all their consorts when they toured Shenyang and their other territories. Only the privileged few chosen by the emperor would have had the opportunity to travel.

Although the Nine Room Pavilion is relatively small when compared with other palace structures, it possesses, just as the sparrow of Chinese proverb possesses every faculty, all the facilities necessary

*Many paintings of door gods, done on paper or silk, have been preserved in Shenyang Palace. Most of these feature the door gods as a pair of fierce generals, but less frequently, they also appear as cherubs.*

*Door gods are hung during the Lunar New Year to protect the palace throughout the year. The origin of this practice has been traced to a story from the Tang dynasty.*

*Emperor Tang Tai Zhong fell ill and was disturbed nightly by the appearance of devils. He became so frightened that he commanded two of his bravest generals to stand guard at the palace doors. This they did, and as a result, the devils no longer haunted the distressed emperor. In order to have continued protection from evil, the emperor commissioned portraits of the generals and ordered the paintings to be pasted on the palace doors. From then onward, the practice of hanging pictures of door gods not only became a tradition of the palace, but also among the households of the common folk.*

for imperial comfort. Thus, the pavilion is an excellent representation of life in the Qing court, and offers a vivid vignette of how the emperor and his ladies lived.

The pavilion has several interesting features. The roof is composed of three stacked awnings, and the plan of the building is a perfect square divided into nine rooms of equal size — nine being the most auspicious of all numbers in Chinese numerology.

Like the palaces in Beijing and Shenyang, the Nine Room Pavilion was heated from below. Wood and charcoal were burnt in a hearth and heat was transferred through a network of ducts below the floorboards. This was a style of heating adopted from Manchuria.

The walls of the rooms are screens of stretched aquamarine voile, forming a maze of adjoining, yet separate rooms. Lit by ornate lanterns and lamps, the translucent screens turned night into day.

**VIEW FROM THE DRESSING ROOM IN THE NINE ROOM PAVILION SHOWING THE IMPERIAL BED CHAMBER AND THE TOILET**

56

Each of the rooms in the pavilion was designed for different purposes. The central chambers which opened to each other were appointed with a couch and a throne. This was where the consorts gave instructions to courtiers and servants, and paid homage to their lord when he visited.

The entrance of the pavilion is flanked on either side by ante-rooms. These are entered by parting silk curtains and stepping through moongates into quiet and elegant areas ideal for a moment's rest.

The connecting room to the west houses a

RECEPTION ROOM OF THE NINE ROOM PAVILION

58

LEFT ANTE-ROOM OF
THE NINE ROOM
PAVILION

RIGHT ANTE-ROOM OF
THE NINE ROOM
PAVILION

**GOLD PLATED ALTAR
VESSELS**
**Average height: 37.5 cm**

*Sets of incense stick holders, candlesticks and incense burner are standard items used on altars during the worship of dieties or ancestors. This set, made of gold plated bronze and engraved with five-clawed dragons, indicates that they were for imperial use.*

Buddhist shrine. The existence of this place of meditation is evidence of the importance of Buddhism to the Qing people. In fact, Buddhism has long been entrenched in Manchu society, and next to Shamanism, was the most practised religion of the Qing dynasty. Many other Buddhist shrines, both grand and humble, can be found in the Shenyang Palace complex. These, with appropriate names such as The Palace of Peaceful Life and The Palace of the Benevolent Alternative, were places where the emperor and his retinue worshipped while they lived in Shenyang.

Moving from the ante-room on the east, one enters, via fan doors, the study where the emperor or his consorts could relax, read or practise calligraphy. Among the Scholar's Four Treasures (inkstick, inkstone, brush and paper) placed on the desk is a red inkstick. Only the emperor wrote in red; everyone else, in black.

The perfume of jasmine and the fragrance of cosmetics waft from the third chamber to the east. This is the dressing room — the most important room to a noble lady of ancient China. Here, the current imperial favourite preened and bedecked herself for the delight of the emperor. The eunuch who combed her hair would be adroit in concealing any strand which dropped off, so as not to evoke the lady's wrath.

Sitting before her dressing table, she would open an exquisite incised silver box and withdraw

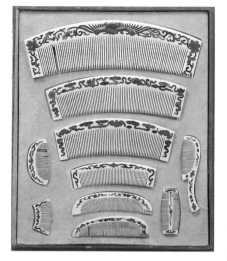

**A SET OF IVORY COMBS**

*For ancient Chinese ladies, hair combing was the most important activity in preparing oneself for the day. The process could take up to an hour.*

*This set of combs of various sizes and fineness helps recapture the scene of maidens, seated before ornate dressing tables, carefully grooming and styling their hair.*

*Ivory was a product of South-east Asia and was considered a luxury item in China.*

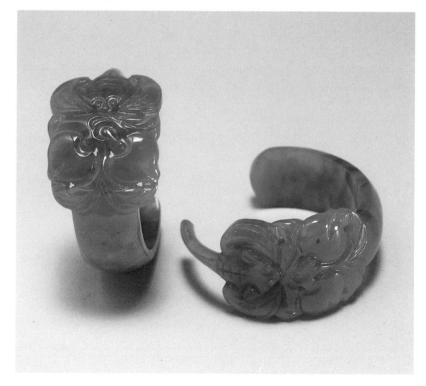

**A PAIR OF JADEITE EARRINGS**
Diameter: 2.5 cm

*Jewellery, like other art forms of the Qing period, often carry Chinese symbols of luck and good fortune. In a simple, yet elegant design, this jeweller has created a pair of ear rings showing bats resting on peaches. The bat (Fu) in the Chinese mind is a harbinger of good things as it puns with the character for beatitude (Fu). Peaches on the other hand, are the ubiquitous symbol for a long and happy life.*

61

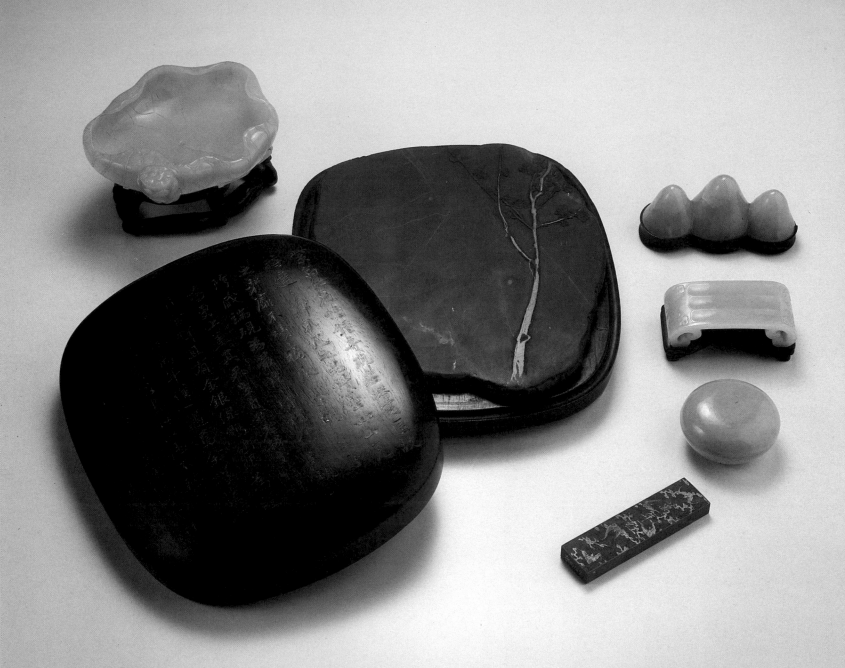

**DUAN INKSTONE**
Length: 24 cm
Width: 19 cm

*The best inkstones from China are from the creek called Duan in Guang-dong province. These Duan stones are unrivalled because they are fine textured, hard and receives the ink without loss through seepage. The carver of this inkstone, inspired by the grain of the stone, added plum blossoms to the 'branch' to create a design which enhances the natural beauty of the piece.*

**RED AND GOLD INKSTICK**
Length: 10 cm

*This red inkstick is made of cinnabar and gilt with gold leaf. Red ink was used exclusively by the emperor. Government and official papers submitted to the throne were all written in black but the emperor, having perused the documents, would write his comments and orders in red ink against the submissions.*

**MILKY WHITE JADE BRUSH REST**
Length: 4 cm
Width: 2 cm
Height: 1.5 cm

*Shaped like three moutains, this piece of nephrite jade from Xin-jiang is where a scholar rests his wet brush during a pause in his writing.*

**YELLOW JADE INK BOX**
Diameter: 5 cm

*Made from yellow jade of Chinese origin, this box contains vermillion ink used for Chinese seals. Chinese scholars applied their seals as signatures to documents. Seals were also used to sign paintings and works of calligraphy done by a scholar himself or in his possession.*

**NEPHRITE JADE INKSTICK STAND**
Length: 8.75 cm
Width: 3.75 cm

*This charming inkstick stand in the shape of a scroll was where an inkstick would be placed when not in use.*

**NEPHRITE JADE DISH**
Length: 5.5 cm
Width: 4.5 cm
Height: 3 cm

*This carved dish of Nephrite from Xinjiang, is in the shape of a curled lotus leaf with a small lotus pod nestling by its side.*

**STUDY IN THE NINE ROOM PAVILION**

63

an ornament. From another ornate jewel box of ivory, she would lift a jade hairpin, place it in her coiffure and adjust the arrangement with an antique comb. A brush of the lashes and a dab on her lips would complete her resplendent beauty.

At the very heart of the pavilion is the imperial bed chamber. Draped with flowing embroidered curtains and plush with silk bolsters, this was the room of dreams.

Story has it that the emperor never went to the women of the palace. He was forbidden to do so. Instead, the names of the candidates would be placed on a tray for his majesty's choice. Disrobed and swathed in silk, the chosen one would be borne on a litter to the imperial bedchamber. After an appropriate interval, the eunuchs would enter and carry the lady away. At that point, the emperor's order was sought if the woman should be allowed to conceive. If so, she was favoured; if not, she suffered a primitive abortion procedure.

Ensuite to the bedchamber is the 'cleansing room' — an euphemism for the imperial toilet. Made of silver or pewter, the bucket was placed below a seat much like the toilet facilities of today. On hot summer days, the 'cool cleansing seat' would be used and when the weather turned chilly and cold, the emperor sat on a seat padded with cushions. Such was the extent of care to ensure imperial comfort.

The emperor and his consorts were served hand and foot by an army of eunuchs and handmaidens. Although these servants worked and lived within the richness of the palace grounds, they were subject to the strictest of restraints.

At the height of Qing power, up to 2,600

**TOILET IN THE NINE ROOM PAVILION**

*This view shows the lounge area of the toilet. The commodes are found in the curtained alcove to the left of the picture.*

**JADEITE HAIRPIN IN THE SHAPE OF A DRAGON'S HEAD**

*Faced with a piece of jadeite from Burma of uneven colour, the jade carver has cleverly used a patch of white to highlight the horns of this dragon head hairpin.*

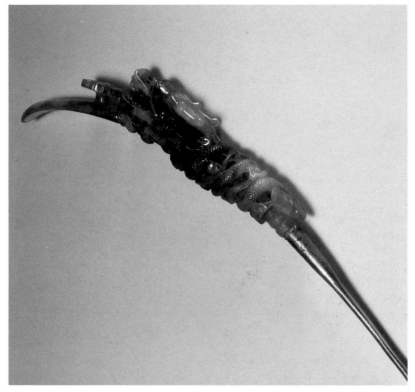

**EMERALD JADE HAIRPIN IN THE SHAPE OF A RU YI**
**Length: 11.8 cm**

*This jade hairpin is of great value because of the quality of the brilliant green jadeite from Burma. It is made in the shape of the Ru Yi, itself a propitious symbol. In addition, the ornament bears a stylised character of the word Shou (longevity) on its head.*

65

**SMALL CABINET WITH JADE PANELS**
Height: 78 cm
Width: 48 cm

*This cabinet is a display on a 'kang', a heated platform made of bricks, which served as a seat by day and a bed at night.*

*The cabinet, made of black sandalwood, is fitted with green jade panels carved with cloud and dragon motifs. The quality of the jade and the refined craftsmanship make this an exceptional piece. It was made specially for imperial use.*

eunuchs served within the walls of the imperial palace. Even at the close of the dynasty, there were 1,600 eunuchs who continued their service. Perhaps the most famous eunuch of all was Li Lianying. He was the henchman of the Empress Dowager Ci Xi during the final years of the Qing period. Much favoured by the aged dowager, he wielded great power and influence in the court.

However, Li Lianying and his pack were rare exceptions. Eunuchs were commonly employed in hard labour and many were worked to death. Those who survived to old age, and were allowed to leave the service of the royal household, fared no better. Marked and mocked, they bore the stigma of castration and became outcasts of society.

**PAGODA-SHAPED INCENSE BURNERS**
Height: 61 cm

*This pair of exquisite incense burners were placed on side tables in the Nine Room Pavilion. Delicately wrought, each of the hexagonal burners have pillars around which are coiled golden dragons. The ceiling of the structure, also in gold, are inlaid with white nephrite jade, as are the railing panels and awning.*

**GARMENT FOR THE EMPEROR**
Length: 134 cm
Skirt length: 111 cm
Sleeve length: 92 cm

*Made of silk brocade, this garment used by the emperor for casual wear, is richly embroidered on the sleeves and collar.*

Eunuchs were sold to the imperial court as young boys by desperate families. Others were the sons and grandsons of criminals and offenders. Because of their age, these boys were spared the death sentence and remained imprisoned till they were made eunuchs at the age of ten.

Handmaidens were chosen annually from the daughters of the imperial household servants. At the age of thirteen, they entered the court to attend to the demands of the imperial ladies. It was not till they passed their twenty-fifth year that they would be allowed to return to their families and be married. In the interim, the girls were virtual slaves, separated from parents and home.

Each day, they silently worked under strict supervision. No sound of laughter passed their lips in the presence of the eminent; no word was

**YELLOW 'KESI' ROBE FOR WOMEN**
Length: 142 cm
Skirt : 117 cm
Sleeve length: 52 cm

*A winter robe for Qing noble women, this 'Kesi' or tapestry weave robe is decorated with heavy blue borders of a fine design.*

spoken beyond a whisper. They laboured, perhaps secretly hoping that one day, they might catch the emperor's eye and strike his fancy. However, in reality, few handmaidens became ladies of title.

When a Qing emperor or a prince married, their consorts must be handpicked from the daughters of their best Bannermen. Once in every three years, young maidens aged thirteen to sixteen were chosen as eligible. Even girls aged seventeen were considered less than perfect and were listed as such. The selection was done by the Administrators of the Royal Household, and from the bevy, they picked brides for the emperor, the princes and other male members of royalty.

Life for the ladies in the imperial court were strictly ordered by a formal hierarchy. And although the princes and princesses they bore for

**GLASS POWDER BOXES**

*For the ancient Chinese, goods imported from the West were as valuable as Chinese art in Europe. This pair of glass powder boxes is a good example. A western import, they were considered very valuable because of their rarity. The nobility went as far as to display such Western goods with their collection of archaic bronzeware.*

69

**HARDWOOD JEWEL BOX
INLAID WITH IVORY**
Height: 34.5 cm
Length: 35 cm
Width: 18.75 cm

*The painted ivory inlay of this wooden jewel box depicts three fruits symbolising good fortune. There are bands of Buddha's fruit on the top and bottom panels of the box while the left and right doors show pomegranate and peach trees respectively. In Chinese tradition, pomegranates represent an abundance of progeny while peaches symbolise longevity.*

the emperor were allowed to remain with them till the children came of age, there was little familiy life except on festive days.

Of course, the emperor had his favourites, and from these he chose those who would accompany him when he went on tour. Thus, here in the exquisite Nine Room Pavilion, the priviledged few counted their blessings and hoped that they would continue to remain foremost in the thoughts of their lord.

## IMPERIAL DINING SET

A daily meal for a Qing emperor consisted of at least 20 to 30 sumptuous courses, for as sovereign, it was his perogative to sample and savour a great many dishes. It is not surprising then, that a large number and wide variety of tablewares, made of gold, silver, jade, porcelain or enamel, were used in at each meal. These included hot pots as well as warming bowls and chafing dishes to keep food hot in the cold winters of northern China.

The emperor had an early meal taken at 6 — 7 in the morning, and a second meal taken at about noon. Throughout the day, he would also be served wine and snacks. Then, towards the evening or at night, the emperor could order a meal at any time according to his fancy.

When the emperor dined, he did not dine at a fixed place, but at whichever pavilion he was visiting. Like the empress and imperial consorts, he always dined alone, except on special occasions

An example of the imperial menu of the 10th day of the New Year, during the 12th year of the reign of Qian Long (1747), clearly shows how lavish royal meals were. That night, it was recorded that the emperor was served:
Bird's nest cooked with shredded young chicken, mushrooms, ham, cabbage and apples, served in a red bowl with wave designs. A dish called Three Immortals — being essentially meat, fish and viscera. Bird's nest with duck and ham. Chicken wings with stewed vegetables and mushrooms prepared by a specialty chef. Plump chicken and Chinese cabbage served in a cloisonne bowl. A rich double-boiled soup. Vegetable stew with wine and white sauce. Sliced duck in a rich soup. Shredded wild fowl with pickled vegetables. Chive shoots stir-fried with shredded venison. Roasted deer. Pan fried dumplings filled with chicken and lamb. Pork and mutton dishes. Imperial style noodles served on a silver platter. Manchurian bean paste dessert. A selection of vegetables and delicacies.

The amount of raw ingredients set aside as the emperor's entitlement was also staggering. This comprised 22 katis of meat for dishes, 5 katis meat for soups, 1 kati of lard, 2 lambs, 5 chicken, 3 ducks, 19 katis Chinese cabbage, spinach, parsley, celery, 60 radishes and carrots, 1 winter melon, 5 katis of vegetables, 6 katis spring onions, 4 taels of wine, 3 katis of sauce, 2 katis of vinegar, 60 buns, 100 katis milk and 10 katis tea leaves. (Note: 1 kati is approx. 650 gsm)

# Treasures of the Qing Dynasty

**LARGE THREE-COLOUR PORCELAIN DISH**
Diameter: 71 cm
Height: 9 cm

*Su San Cai (plain three-colour porcelain), mainly in purple, green and yellow was popular during the reign of Kang Xi. Although made specifically for imperial use at Jingdezhen, a dish of this size was a rarity even in the palace since such large pieces required great technical skill to produce.*

The art and craft of any age directly reflects the political, social and economic conditions, and thinking of that society. It is true that craftsmen have technical control over the production of *objets d'art*, but ultimately, it is still the needs and taste of their patrons — monarch, scholar and artistic supervisor — that determine the style and design of the work.

The political upheavels that so deeply affected 17th century China has left its mark on the art and craft of the period. The banditry and civil strife which ravaged the country at the close of the Ming era destroyed production facilities and wreaked havoc on nearly every type of Chinese handicraft. The imperial porcelain produced in Jingdezhen, for instance, showed a sharp decline in both quality and quantity during those years.

It was thus not till the reign of Kang Xi that peace and prosperity once again brought the flourishing of decorative art in China.

In the 150 years between 1654 and 1799, covering the rule of Kang Xi, Yong Zheng and Qian Long, decorative art enjoyed an unprecedented period of growth.

The Manchus had no deep-rooted cultural traditions of their own, and eager to cement their position as rulers under the 'Mandate of Heaven', adopted many Chinese beliefs and practices. These ranged from subscribing to the most reactionary

*This lovely jade chime is styled after the stone chimes popular during China's bronze age. It is hung in a delicately carved black sandalwood stand bearing a pair of phoenixes.*

76

**CLOISONNE VASE IN
THE SHAPE OF AN
ARCHAIC BRONZE VASE**
**Height: 23 cm**
**Width at mouth: 7.5 cm**

forms of Confucianism to the use of ritual vessels copied from archaic bronzeware. During this period, large quantities of porcelain, carved laquerware, jade and cloisonne were made according to ancient designs. Examples of these can be seen in the cloisonne vase, jade disc and jade chime shown in this exhibition. This return to archaism reflected the generally conservative mood of the society and the Manchu's search for public approval.

*Like this small cloisonne vase, many artefacts from the Qing dynasty were made in the style of archaic bronze ware or jade ritual ornaments. This fashion reflects the Manchu desire foracceptance by the Han Chinese by following the most conservative forms of Confucionism.*

At the same time, under direct Manchu influence, decorative art departed from the simpler Ming style and tended towards heavy ornamentation. Likewise, the use of a vibrant and wide palette may be attributed to the Manchu's taste for strong colours. During this period, utensils of Manchu and Mongolian origins — like the ornate Mongolian ewer — were also introduced into the essentially Chinese repertoire.

Hence, in art as in politics, the Qing period was an age of strong conservatism. All energy expended on art and craft were directed at pursuing technical perfection rather than creativity and innovation. From this, and government support, the technical skill of Qing craftsmen and the complexity of their design work reached a zenith.

Unlike the corrupt Ming system where eunuchs were sent to indiscriminately order art objects for the court, the Qing imperial household provided financial assistance and ensured that craftsmen were given down-payments to provide the necessary stability for them to concentrate on their work. Scholar supervisors were also appointed to the workshops, leading to better organisation and more refined designs.

Factories were established to supply the needs of royalty, mandarin and gentry. Imperial porcelain continued to be produced in Jingdezhen while Suzhou, Hangzhou and Nanjing supplied the finest embroideries. Fuzhou offered painted lacquerware and Beijing excelled in carved lacquer and cloisonne products.

Qing art, besides benefitting from government control, also gained much from royal patronage. The evidence of decorative objects used by emper-

**GOLD LACQUERED FRUIT CONTAINERS DECORATED WITH PINE LEAVES**
Height: 62.5 cm
Width: 35 cm

*The motif of this unusual and stunning pair of fruit containers is the mythical dragon. Besides being used on the roof and base, the beasts are cleverly linked to coil around the vessel.*

79

or and monarch is particularly strong in this exhibition. Many articles on display — porcelain, woodcarvings and textile — are decorated with dragons, signifying the emperor and his power.

Emperor Kang Xi went to the extent of setting up workshops within the palace precinct for the manufacture of, among other things, porcelain, laquerware, furniture as well as glass, enamel and jade objects for royalty. These workshops, employing the best craftsmen of the realm, not surprisingly produced some of the most outstanding examples of Qing decorative art.

**PORCELAIN JAR WITH DRAGON IN OVERGLAZED GREEN**
**Height: 21 cm**
**Widest diameter: 15 cm**

*Although dragons were common designs in imperial ware, this jar is made unusual by the fact that the design is in overglazed green when motifs on such vessels were normally painted in underglazed cobalt blue.*

As in the imperial workshops, craftsmen in other centres throughout the country reached heights of technical excellence and virtuosity. But there was close supervision, and motifs and shapes of art pieces were restricted. This was a direct result of the autocratic style of government adopted by the Qing emperors, who, as foreigners who ruled China, sought to take control of the thinking of the people in every way.

In this effort, there was also a large-scale purge on the malcontent elements of the literati. Some scholars had, after the fall of the Ming, expressed their desire for the restoration of the old kingdom through their poems and essays. To squelch these elements, the Manchus occupied the literati in collecting, compiling and copying a massive library covering the entire range of published works in China.

This exertion of energy, in the final analysis, can only be considered a waste of manpower. Similarly, in the pursuit of technical excellence, Qing art tended towards over-decoration. Essays of thousands of words would be squeezed onto a rice grain and a humble olive stone would be carved with scenes from an entire drama.

In terms of motifs and designs employed in decoration, there was a strong religious influence on Manchus taste. The Manchus and Mongols were devout Buddhists, and Taoism, which had taken deep root during the Ming period, had also influenced their thinking. Hence, Qing art is often decorated with the pantheon of Taoist mythology and Buddhist symbols. Examples of these are the motifs of the peach of longevity, cranes, bats and gourds — all pointing to the Chinese desire for Fu

(beatitude), Lu (wealth) and Shou (longevity).

Among the exhibits, one can see evidence of this in the nine peach porcelain vase, the design of bats on the red silk garment, cranes on the ladies' gown and the Taoist god of longevity on an ivory brush holder.

In perspective, the spectrum of Qing decorative art did not far exceed what the Ming had accomplished. The Ming achievements in art and craft, namely porcelain, carved laquerware and cloisonne, continued to excel during the Qing period, and such excellence, under Manchu rule, brought the development of technical skill to points never reached in the history of Chinese art.

**IVORY BRUSH HOLDER**
Height: 20 cm
Diameter: 10.6 cm

*Carved from one piece of ivory, this brush holder depicts a fairy presenting books to the god of longevity, recognised here by his long eyebrows. The sculptor has given the god a gentle smile and has carved his hands clasped in appreciation, reflecting the benevolence and wisdom of the diety.*

**POLYCHROME ENAMEL PORCELAIN VASE WITH NINE PEACHES**
Largest diameter: 38 cm
Height: 52 cm

*According to Chinese symbolism, nine is the number of abundance, and peaches are associated with birthdays. Thus, the nine peaches on this vase together symbolise longevity. It was made at the imperial kiln at Jingdezhen during the reign of Emperor Qian Long. Perhaps this elegant vase was a birthday gift to a member of the royal family.*

82

## EMBROIDERED RED SILK GARMENT FOR THE EMPRESS

**Length: 139 cm**
**Skirt length: 116 cm**
**Sleeve length: 108 cm**

*Made of plain weave silk and gorgeously embroidered with a hundred bats to symbolise happiness, this garment is characteristic of the outer robes worn by Qing noble women during spring and autumn.*

## EMBROIDERED WOOLEN FEMALE GARMENT

**Length: 145 cm**
**Width: 110 cm**
**Sleeve length: 96 cm**

*Made of a woollen fabric from Russia, this gown, finely embroidered with white cranes, was worn in spring and autumn by ladies of the Qing court.*

83

# PORCELAIN

From the viewpoint of art history, Chinese porcelain reached its high point during the reigns of Kang Xi, Yong Zheng and Qian Long. Porcelain produced by the imperial kilns during this period has never been surpassed.

With an unlimited supply of Kaolin (porcelain clay) at Jingdezhen in Jiangxi province, tens of thousands of craftsmen worked in the heat of some ten thousand kilns to produce porcelain ware which far surpassed the efforts of their Ming counterparts. Encouraged by government funding and supervised by scholars, the craftsmen of this 150-year period achieved breakthroughs in technique, especially in the diversity of glaze colours.

Even today, it is difficult to duplicate some of the finest monochrome products of the Kang Xi period. These include copper-red (*sang-de-boeuf*),

**DOU CAI JAR**
**Height: 12 cm**
**Diameter: 11.25 cm**

*Painted with underglazed blue and overglazed yellow and red, this porcelain jar is decorated with tendril designs and medallions of chrysanthemums.*

**POLYCHROME ENAMEL PORCELAIN MONGOLIAN MILK JAR**
**Height: 47 cm**
**Diameter: 14.8 cm**

*The polychrome enamel technique of decorating porcelain was an innovation during the Qing dynasty. Outlines of designs, drawn by a traditional Chinese brush technique, were filled with glazed colours, achieving a subtle shading to give a three-dimensional effect. At the same time, the motifs are well-defined and highlighted by the fine outlines.*

*This Mongolian-style milk jar reflects the closeness of the Manchus with the Mongolian people. The dragon on the handle and the phoenix design on the spout indicates that it was made for imperial use. The vessel, which has a lion sitting arrogantly on its lid, is decorated with lotus blooms and the eight Buddhist treasures.*

*These show the extent of Buddhist influence on both the Manchu and Mongolian people.*

85

**FIVE-COLOUR (WU CAI) PORCELAIN MEI-PING VASE DECORATED WITH DRAGON AND PHEONIX**
Shoulder diameter: 23 cm
Height: 43.5 cm

*An imperial ware, this vase is a product of Jing-dezhen during the Yong Zheng period. It is a fine example of Wu Cai or Five Colour porcelain where brilliant over-glazed and underglazed colours are applied on the bisque. This piece vividly captures the spirit of the dragon and phoenix — the former being the symbol for the emperor and the latter, the empress — as they dance joyously among designs of leaves and flowers.*

the 'mottled' and powdered blues, egg-shell white, as well as the range of yellow derived from iron, ochre, sienna and burnt umber.

Even more widely admired are the Kang Xi blue-and-white glaze, and the polychrome enamel ware which blossomed during this period. The *famille verte* and *famille rose* techniques of the Yong Zheng and Qian Long periods, with their infinite shades of colour and diversity of attractive designs, will continue to evoke admiration.

Perhaps not so widely published are the *Duo Cai* ware. *Duo Cai*, which literally means unglazed blue 'fighting to be beautiful against overglazed enamel', was a technique experimented by the Ming, but perfected only during the Qing dynasty.

A number of fine examples of *Duo Cai* porcelain are shown in this exhibition. They include the five-coloured phoenix and dragon vase manufactured during the Yong Zheng period, and the exquisite Kang Xi blue-and-white vase over-glazed with purple.

**SMALL BLUE-AND-WHITE VASE WITH OVER GLAZED PURPLE**
Height: 14.5 cm
Diameter: 9 cm

*This vase was a Jing-dezhen imperial ware made during the Kang Xi period when blue-and-white porcelain with over glazed purple designs were very popular. The technique works well in this example, giving the design a quiet beauty.*

## CLOISONNE

Cloisonne is an important art form of ancient China comparable, to a certain extent, with porcelain in terms of popularity.

The technique of producing cloisonne originated from Persia and was introduced to China early in the Ming dynasty. The process involves filling designs, outlined by bronze wire welded onto a bronze object, with different coloured enamels. High heat would then be applied to melt and fuse the enamel onto the bronze. This process would be repeated several times before the final polishing brought out the brilliance of the multi-coloured cloisonne.

Although cloisonne making was an imported art form, all traces of foreign elements have long since disappeared from the designs. Instead, the cloisonne technique was applied in the Qing period to the most classical of Chinese styles. An example of a cloisonne vessel shaped like an archaic bronze vessel is shown in this exhibition.

In this art form, the Qings concentrated on applying the technique on an ever increasing variety of daily objects rather than improving the technique itself. Thus, examples of cloisonne exhibited include not only vases and a panel decorated with peonies, but also ritual objects placed in front of the imperial throne.

**DECORATIVE PANEL WITH INLAID CLOISONNE PEONIES**
**Height: 210 cm**
**Width: 90 cm**

*The typical colour used in cloisonne ware is blue, and this panel — with pink and red peonies — is more unusual for it. The technical excellence of the piece show how the craftsmanship of cloisonne ware had developed during the middle of the Qing dynasty.*

Nephrite. Nephrite jade is mainly green or white. The latter, known as 'mutton fat jade' was particularly favoured by Chinese scholars because of its pure creamy colouring.

Jadeite, commonly used in Chinese jewelry, became popular only during the Qing dynasty. Mined in the area between Yunnan and northern Burma, the best jadeite is *Fei Cui*, a name which describes the translucent green lustre of the jade.

Jade in the Qing dynasty was mainly used to make ornaments or ritual objects. Here, the very imperial seal which recognises the emperor's power to rule under the 'Mandate of Heaven' is made of jade. So too, the history and geneology of the dynasty are carved on jade tablets. This was because jade was believed to have enduring — even everlasting — qualities. For the same reason, ritual objects are commonly carved of jade, and these are

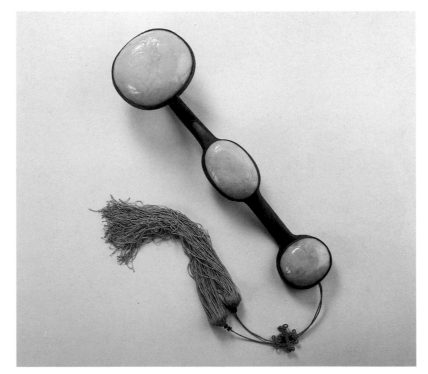

**RU YI INLAID WITH WHITE JADE**
**Length: 45 cm**

*The Ru Yi was originally a back scratching instrument which gradually evolved into a symbol of good luck. Ru Yi were particulary popular during the Qing dynasty when it was presented as a gift to superior persons and placed on one's seat as a decorative item. Inlaid with three pieces of 'mutton fat' nephrite jade from Xinjiang, it is carved lightly with leaf designs. The elegance of this Ru Yi is enhanced by the addition of two tassels and a Chinese knot.*

91

often made in the most classical of styles. The three-legged incense burner and the incense burner in the shape of a mythical animal shown here are fine examples of this treatment.

Jade was also lavishly used to make objects of daily use for the imperial court. The emperor ate out of jade bowls and his library was equipped with brush rests, water containers, scroll boxes and seal boxes — all made of precious jade.

Where the Ming tended towards smooth, rounded designs and simple lines in their jade carving, the craftsmen of the Qing period applied their skill and imagination on the precious stone to produce works of intricate beauty.

As such, a hairpin of emerald jade would show the soft hand of a maiden carrying delicate flowers, or a piece of white jade would be transformed into a vase depicting a magnolia bud caught at the moment of perfection as its petals opened to release sweet perfume.

**JADEITE HAIRPIN OF HAND HOLDING A FLOWER BASKET**

*There is subtle humour in this exquisite hairpin of a hand holding flowers and a basket. It not only shows the originality and imagination of the jeweller, but also hints at his wit and personality.*

*A little tongue in cheek, he adds a jade bangle around the wrist of the hand, making sure that this hairpin, which no doubt will add to the accessories on a heavily bejewelled lady, is also in itself, bejewelled.*

**JADE INCENSE BURNER**
Height: 21.25 cm
Diameter at widest: 13.75 cm

*Two young lions prance energetically on the lid of this incense burner made from jade of Chinese origin. The ears of the vessel are in the shape of mystical animal heads. The tongues of the creatures reach down to the bowl, holding a pair of rings.*

92

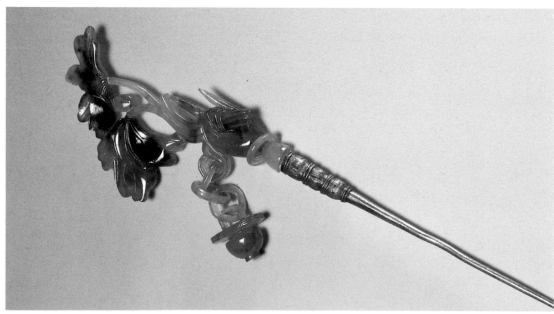

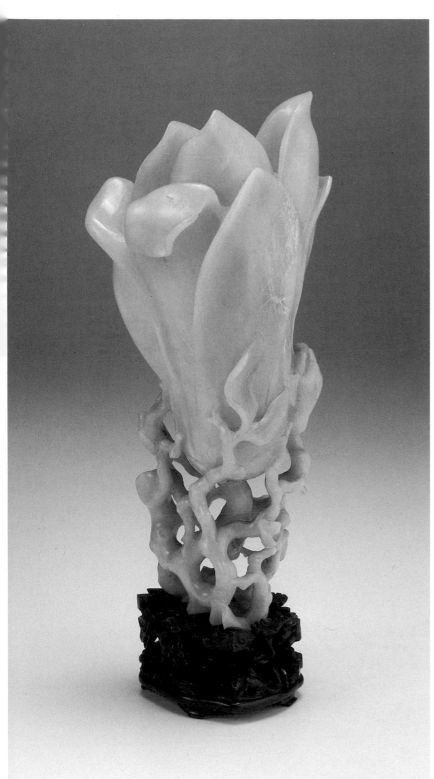

## JADE VASE IN THE FORM OF MAGNOLIA FLOWER

**Height: 25.3 cm**
**Diameter of mouth: 10.7 cm**

*This elegant and valuable vase in the shape of a magnolia blossom is carved from a piece of choice white nephrite jade. The sculptor has captured the flower as it passed from bud to bloom, and one can well imagine the fragrance of magnolia scent filling the room in which this delightful vase stands.*

## JADE CONTAINER DECORATED WITH LANDSCAPE AND

**Height: 9 cm**
**Diameter: 7.5 cm**

*The scene carved on this small container made from jade of Chinese origin is alive with energy. Deeply incised such that the picture conveys the feeling of being completely three dimensional, the figures and landscape, while not executed in exact detail, nonetheless give the impression of vigour and life.*

## JADE CIRCULAR TABLE SCREEN
**Diameter: 14 cm**

*The view carved on this jade table screen is a haunting landscape devoid of people. The row of trees on the horizon adds a dimension of mystery to this quiet scene.*

*The jade is of Chinese origin while the stand is made of black sandalwood imported from South-east Asia.*

## JADE INCENCE BURNER IN THE SHAPE OF A MYTHICAL ANIMAL
**Height: 25 cm**
**Length: 24 cm**

*This mythical creature symbolised loyalty, righteousness and wisdom, and incense burners made in its form were always placed as an ornament in front of the emperor's throne. The beast represented a loyal and wise official, and was placed before the throne to ward off craftiness and deceit.*

94

### CHINESE JADE CANDLESTICK IN THE SHAPE OF A BIRD
**Height: 23.75 cm**
**Width: 12.5 cm**

*This whimiscal candles-tick shows a bird stand-ing on a tortoise. The water fowl has its wings spread, as if balancing itself while the tortoise moves slowly along.*

### WHITE JADE DISH
**Diameter: 20 cm**
**Height: 9.6 cm**

*Made of mutton-fat nephrite from Xinjiang, this translucent, cream-coloured dish glows with understated elegence. It has a pair of ears in the shape of animal heads, each holding a ring light-ly in their mouths.*

### JADE BOX WITH PINE AND CRANE MOTIFS
**Diamater: 21.25 cm**
**Height: 17 cm**

*Finely carved from jade of Chinese origin, this box has a design of pines and cranes — both sym-bols of longevity. The box is also inlaid with a piece of 'mutton fat' nephrite from Xinjiang.*

97

## EMBROIDERY AND WEAVING

Chinese embroidery is characterised by intricate needlework and the ability to blend different coloured threads to produce pictures as detailed and vivid as paintings.

Although sericulture originated in northern China, the centre of silk production and embroidery moved with time to the south. In fact, in the Ming dynasty, Suzhou — as it still remains today — had already become the centre well known for embroidery.

The Qing emperors established three main embroidery workshops in Nanjing, Suzhou and Hangzhou. These were manned by imperial servants who also spied out rebel elements for the emperor.

In fact, Cao Xueqin, the author of the Chinese classic, *The Dream of the Red Chamber*, was a grandson of the chief embroidery supervisor at Nanjing. It is therefore not surprising that his work contains detailed descriptions of the lavish fabrics, embroidery and decorations used in the styles of dress fashionable in those days. In particular, there are many references to the embroidered aromatic pouches, purses and fan cases in vogue among both Qing nobility and common folk.

In this exhibition, we have excellent examples of fine embroidery and weaving on silk, wool and brocade. There are also examples of silk tapestry weave and a lovely collection of embroidered pouches.

**FEMALE GARMENT DECORATED WITH SIGNS OF LONGEVITY**
Length: 134 cm
Skirt length: 112 cm
Sleeve length: 61 cm

*This silk gauge summer dress is of the type worn by women of the Qing court. It is decorated with twill-weave roundels of the Chinese character for longevity.*

98

### POUCHES, PURSES AND FAN COVERS

*Embroidered aromatic pouches, purses and fan cases were popular items carried by the nobility and common folk during the Qing dynasty. These were exchanged as gifts during the festive season and were also used as tokens of engagement by lovers.*

*Originating from a culture where hunting played an important social role, the Manchus were particularly fond of pouches which they used to store food, knives, flints and other necessities of an outdoor life. When they settled in China and chose a more leisurely lifestyle, the pouches became smaller and were used to contain aromatic, herbal items.*

*The pair of mottled brown pouches shown here is made of deer hide. During the reign of Qian Long, he specifically ordered that such pouches be made of deer skin to remind his people of the more austere life of their ancestors.*

*A fine example of Suzhou embroidery, this panel was made in the middle of the Qing period. It depicts the phoenix, the king of birds, being worshipped by a hundred birds.*

## CARVED LACQUER

The best of Qing lacquerware were made in the 18th century during the reign of Qian Long.

The making of carved lacquerware involved a painstaking process. Craftsmen would apply 20 to 30 layers of lacquer, a layer at a time, onto a base of metal or wood. A good piece of lacquerware is thus identified by its thick layer of brilliant red lacquer — the colour being achieved by adding cinnabar to the liquid lacquer. When the lacquer solidified, the surface would then be carved with detailed landscapes or figures.

100

**CARVED LACQUER BRUSH BOX**
Length: 34 cm
Width: 19 cm
Height: 23 cm

*The brilliant red and thick lacquer indicates that this is a very fine example of Qing red-lacquer ware. The doors of the box are carved with a scene of a river-side, with an intricate repeated lattice design representing water.*

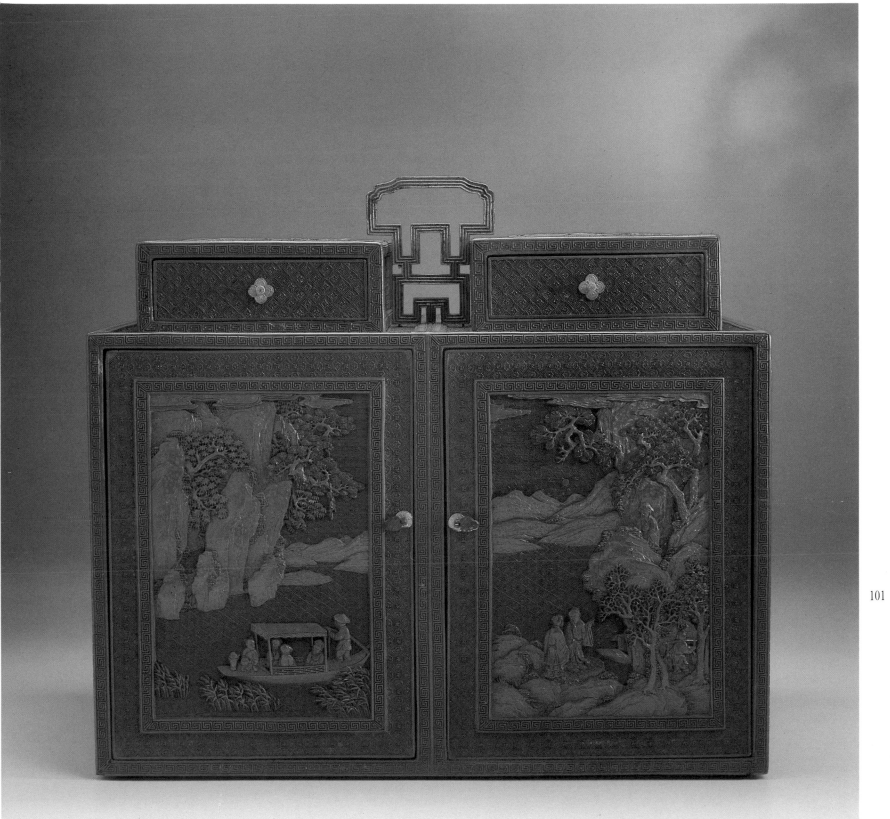

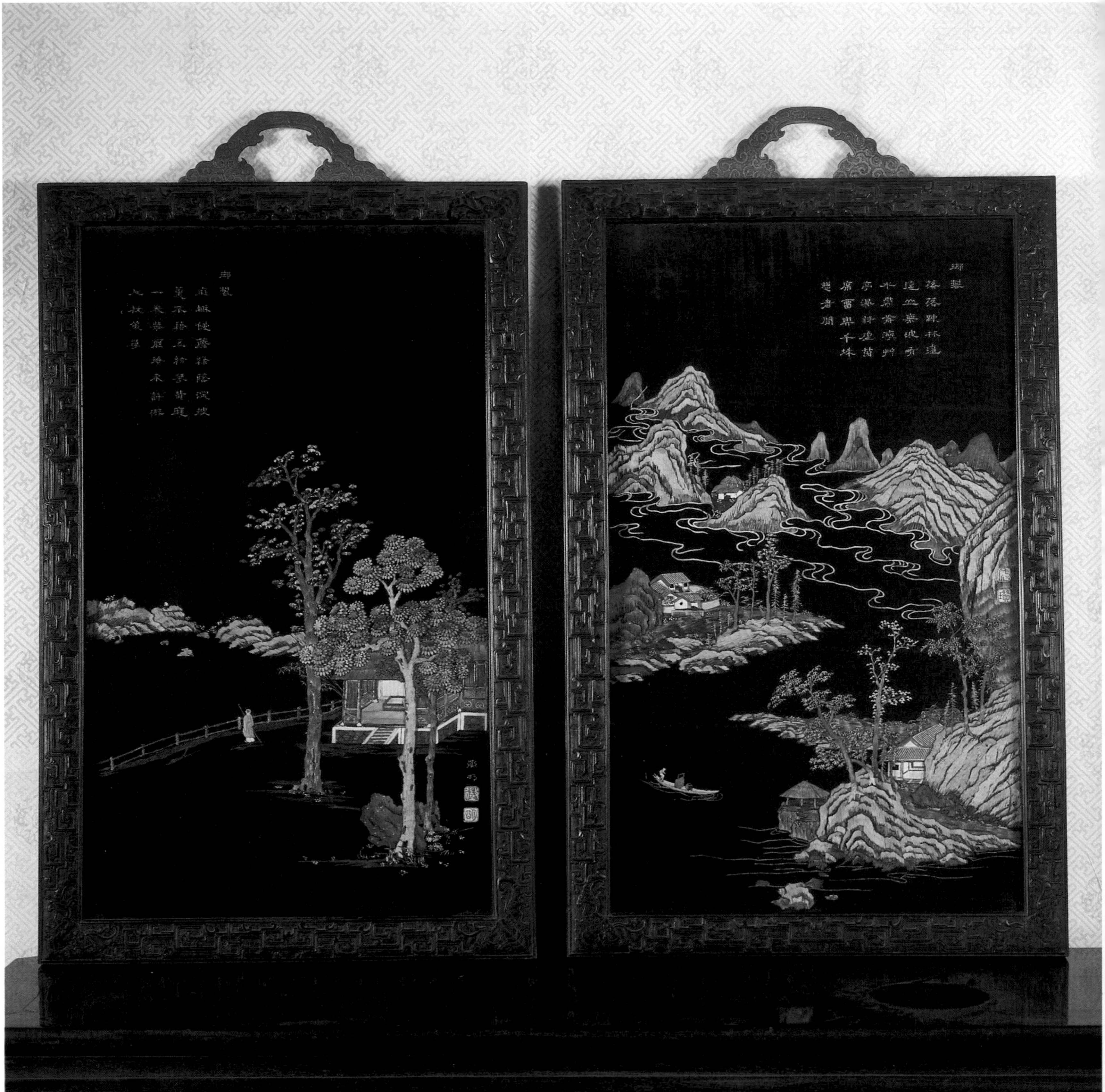

御製
御製

# FEATHER INLAID ART

**DECORATIVE PANELS INLAID WITH KINGFISHER FEATHERS**
Height: 85 cm
Width: 54 cm

*This pair of panels show restful scenes of a hermit's mountain retreat and a mist-covered river. The kingfisher feathers do not only colour the trees and mountains depicted in the picture, but also the characters of the accompanying poems.*

The Chinese were the only people in the world to use kingfisher feathers as an inlay for their jewelry and ornaments. Examples of headgear, inlaid with kingfisher feathers and designed for empresses, have been found in the Ming tombs. Such crowns are known as 'phoenix headgears', showing that the Chinese valued the brilliant feathers of the kingfisher as a worthy substitute for the feathers of the mythical bird. Kingfisher feathers were collected from Guangdong province and South-east Asia.

In the two decorative panels shown in the exhibition, the electric blue kingfisher feathers are used against a jet black background to create restful scenes.

# CHINESE PAINTING AND CALLIGRAPHY

As in other Chinese art and craft, brush painting and calligraphy in the Qing court drew inspiration from earlier Chinese dynasties. To gain acceptance of those they ruled, the Manchu emperors adopted the scholarly pursuits of the Han Chinese. They learnt calligraphy and painting, and the styles they favoured were often copies of Chinese grandmasters. This notwithstanding, the Qing rulers became proficient artists.

One advance made in Chinese painting during the Qing dynasty was the development of painting sans brush. Gao Qipei, a high-ranking official of the Qing court, founded the technique of finger painting and was skillful in producing energetic paintings of landscapes, figures, animals and flowers by using his fingers, palms and hand.

**FINGER PAINTING BY
GUO QIPEI
(EAGLE ON A PINE TREE)**
Length: 292 cm
Width: 75 cm

*With wings poised to launch into flight, the eagle in this powerful painting was drawn with bold, strong strokes. The artist adds two birds in the corner, and in a few deft strokes, captures the panic as the birds flee from imminent attack.*

104

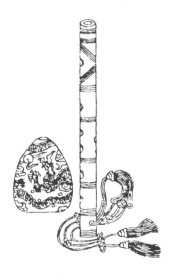

**FINGER PAINTING BY GAO QIPEI (MANDARIN DUCKS IN A POND)**
**Length: 184 cm**
**Width: 97 cm**

*Gao Qipei (1672 — 1734), a high ranking official in the Qing Ministry of Home Affairs is better known today as the founder of finger painting. He developed the technique over a decade and was skillful in the painting of figures, animals, insects and flowers. Gao not only used his fingers as a brush, but also used his palm and the back of his hands.*

**FINGER PAINTING BY GUO QIPEI (OBSERVING THE WATERFALL)**
Length: 410 cm
Width: 151 cm

*This large painting depicts the forces of nature in the roaring waves and rushing water of a river as it plummets from the mountains. In contrast, two men and their servant are on the rocks above, placidly observing the raging torrent.*

**CALLIGRAPHY BY EMPEROR KANG XI**
Length: 297.5 cm
Width: 80 cm

*Kang Xi, the second Manchu emperor, was an exceptional leader with great military prowess and scholastic interests. During his 61-year reign, China was unified and her boundaries extended from Taiwan to Outer Mongolia. While the remaining Ming loyalists were conquered on the battlefield, Ming literati were embraced by the Manchu court and traditional writing and painting flourished. This calligraphy, modelled on the style of Ming calligrapher Dong Qichang (1555 — 1636), is a fine example of Kang Xi's own elegant and scholarly work.*

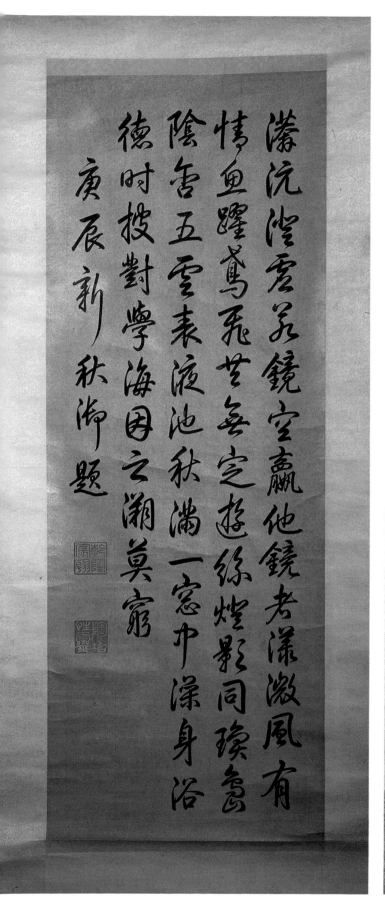

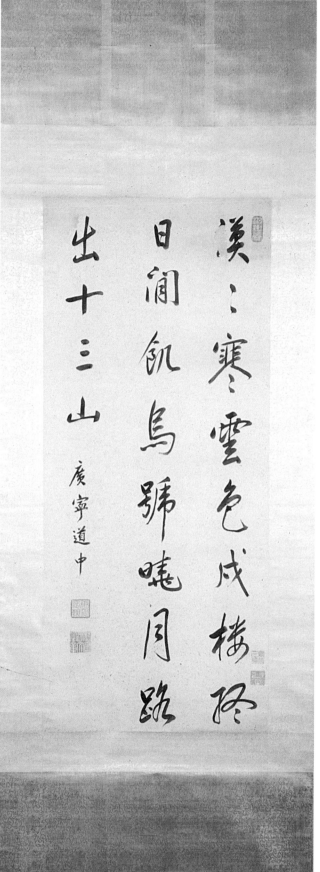

**CALLIGRAPHY BY EMPEROR QIAN LONG**
Length: 225 cm
Width: 97.5 cm

*Emperor Qian Long (1736 — 1795) was an avid lover of art, and his collection of masterworks of Chinese painting and calligraphy from earlier dynasties formed the foundation of the Imperial Palace collection.*

*His calligraphy is smooth and rounded, and was modelled after the style of the Song dynasty calligrapher, Mi Fei.*

107

## INFLUENCE FROM THE WEST

Against a background of great technical achievement, the decorative art and craft of the Qing period can also be discussed in another perspective. This is the fact that during this period, especially from Qian Long onwards, Chinese craftsmen began to produce art and craft for the export market on a commercial scale.

Although Chinese porcelain had been an export item to South-east Asia and the Arabian world since the Tang dynasty (618 — 907), it was Qing porcelain which consolidated the Chinese craft market in Europe and made Chinese porcelain an export commodity of worldwide renown.

Western influence into the world of Chinese art can be traced to the Jesuit priests that entered the service of the early Qing emperors. However, it was Castiglione, an accomplished European painter in the service of the Emperor Qian Long, who introduced perspective and colour shading to Chinese brush paintings.

This technique of shading was later adapted for polychrome enamel porcelain, especially *famille verte* and *famille rose*.

As demand for export porcelain increased, the kilns at Jingdezhen began to produce 'china' according to western taste. European customers went to the extent of sending to Canton, not only specimen shapes, but also specific subjects and designs for decoration. As a result, shipments of Qing porcelain began to emerge with western figures and portraits, hunting scenes and even religious images. This last category of export porcelain is appropriately known as 'Jesuit China'.

It is not a lack of scholarship that studies of Qing art and craft often stop at the end of the Qian Long period. The reason is that the output during the later Qing periods tended to be repetitive of early Qing designs.

Indeed, later Qing craftsmen continued to produce technically beautiful products for the export trade, but with an indifferent and weakened government, the refinement and imagination characteristic of early Qing work quickly faded with the waning of the dynasty.

# 中国沈阳故宫

值此，中华人民共和国沈阳故宫博物院在新加坡共和国举办的《沈阳故宫博物院清代宫廷历史文物展览》开幕之际，我谨代表沈阳故宫博物院向友好的新加坡人民以及各方观众致以诚挚的谢意和良好的祝愿。

铁玉钦
中国沈阳故宫博物院院长

沈阳故宫是清朝入关前的皇宫和入关后皇帝东巡时驻跸的行宫，也是中国除北京故宫之外唯一保存完好的古代宫殿建筑群。现在的沈阳故宫博物院，就是以这处建筑群为基址开辟的。

沈阳故宫的建立，与满族的兴起和建国有着密切的关系。满族是居住在中国东北地区的古老民族。她的先世分别称为肃慎、挹娄、勿吉、靺鞨、女真，并曾建立过金王朝。明代末年，女真人主要分为建州、海西、"野人"三个部落集团。明朝万历十一年（1583年）居住于今辽宁新宾地区的建州女真部爱新觉罗家族的努尔哈赤，起兵攻打他的仇人尼堪外兰。其后势力逐渐强大，统一了女真各部。明万历四十三年（1615年）创立了八旗制度。次年，努尔哈赤于赫图阿拉（今辽宁省新宾满族自治县永陵镇）称"汗"，建国号曰"金"，史称"后金"，这一年也就是后金的天命元年。此后，后金的势力不断扩大，并开始进攻明朝的统治地区，先后占领了抚顺、沈阳、辽阳等要地。辽河以东大小七十余城堡也都归其所有，后金政权的统治中心也随之移到辽沈地区。后金天命六年（1621年）在辽阳旧城之东建造了新城和官室殿宇，第二年把国都迁到了这里，称为"东京城"。三年后，努尔哈赤经过深思熟虑，觉得沈阳水陆交通都很畅通，无论从将来的军事发展还是物资供应都很有利。于是毅然决定将都城由辽阳迁到沈阳。天命十年（1625年）三月初三日，努尔哈赤从辽阳出发，翌日抵达沈阳，从这时到清朝入关，二十年间这里一直是后金（清）的都城。

沈阳是一座有七千多年历史的古城，战国时期为燕国的侯城，辽、金时期称为沈州。元代时始称沈阳，明朝在这里建立沈阳中卫。

砖砌内城外廓，东西南北四座城门，城内十字大街，建有官廨、庙宇、店铺、民居。后金国迁都到这里后，便着手于城中营建新的宫殿——这就是沈阳故宫历史的开端。

沈阳故宫从1625年开始兴建到后金天聪六年（1632年）已经基本建成，崇德元年（1636年）确定了各宫殿的名称，即现存的故宫东路和中路建筑。它座落于明、清沈阳旧城的中心，以沈阳城的南北中轴线为界分为东西两部分。东侧为大政殿和十王亭，是一组很有时代特点和民族特点的建筑。其北部正中为主体建筑——大政殿早期称作"大衙门"或"笃恭殿"，始建于努尔哈赤时期，是当时后金（清）政权举行重大典礼和诸王贝勒大臣商议国家政事的地方。它是一座八角重檐攒尖顶的亭式殿，所以习惯上也称之为"八角殿"或"八方亭"。整个建筑座落于1.5米高的"须弥"台基之上，四周用木制隔扇门而不砌砖石，外檐为五踩双下昂斗拱，正面两檐柱上饰以木雕金漆双龙，殿顶铺黄琉璃饰绿剪边。殿内为"彻上明造"，正中为金漆降龙藻井，周围有汉文和梵文组成的天花，体现了汉、满、蒙、藏等多民族建筑艺术风格。大政殿前东西两侧对称排列着十座方亭，俗称"十王亭"。距大政殿最近的北面两座分别为左、右翼王亭，其它八座称八旗亭，由北至南依次为镶黄、正黄、正白、正红、镶白、镶红、正兰、镶兰，每旗一座。最南端东西各有奏乐亭一座。这样，以大政殿为中心，十王亭为两翼共同构成一个完整的建筑布局，体现了八旗组织在后金（清）国家中的重要地位，在历朝的宫殿建筑中独具特色。

沈阳故宫的中路，旧时称为"大内宫阙"，可以称作宫殿区。建成于清太宗天聪年间。宫殿的正门称"大清门"，为五间硬山式建筑。其南面两侧有奏乐亭，供在此举行典礼时奏乐之用。朝房和朝楼是官员们集会，候朝之处。大清门的东西两边各有一座牌楼，西侧为"武功坊"，东侧为"文德坊"，均建于崇德二年(1637年)。它们实际上相当于宫前的左右阙门，进宫朝见的文武官员必须在牌楼外出轿下马。大清门之北是崇政殿，俗称"金銮殿"，是清入关前沈阳故宫举行日常朝会的地方。殿为五间硬山前后廊式建筑，前后均饰有石雕栏板和瑞兽、抱鼓等，殿两侧墀头、博风板和正脊均用五彩琉璃件装饰，殿内亦为"彻上明造"，望板梁枋上饰有白云、仙桃等彩绘。现在的殿内置有乾隆年间制作的金漆堂陛和屏风宝座。殿前的月台和日晷、嘉量也是乾隆年间增补的。崇政殿东西两侧有左右翼门各三间，殿后高台上是清太宗时期的帝后居住区。它的门户是一座歇山顶三滴水式的三层楼阁——凤凰楼，其中层和上层供皇帝后妃休息、读书、宴饮之用，下层则为进入台上宫区的通道，前有石阶通往台下。凤凰楼后面的宫区共有五座宫殿。正中一座是清宁宫，也称"中宫"，是清太宗皇太极与皇后博尔济吉特氏居住的寝宫，也是宫中举行萨满祭祀的地方。这座建筑有着鲜明的民族特点，它的面阔为五间，从东次间开门，入内后隔开的东梢间是寝宫，其它四间成为"口袋房"式的家祭神堂，宫内有南、西、北三面相连的"蔓枝炕"，西炕上供神位，南北炕既可供人坐寝，又是取暖设施。清宁宫的烟囱不是砌在房顶，而是在宫后西侧的地面上垂直竖起，高过房檐，通过烟道与屋内火炕相连。宫前东南侧，还竖有祭神用的索伦杆子。这些都是满族传统的建筑特色。清宁宫前东西两侧各有四座宫，是清太宗的四位妃子们居住的地方，分别称为关睢宫、麟

趾宫、衍庆宫、永福宫，其中住在永福宫的庄妃布木布泰(蒙古科尔沁部博尔济吉特氏)是清世祖福临(顺治皇帝)的生母，这座宫也是福临的诞生之处。

除了上述这些主要建筑外，早期建筑中还有粮仓、碾房、磨房以及一些存储肉、果、蜜、银两、布匹等用的库房，大部分分布于宫殿四周，以供宫中日常生活所需。直至清朝入关以前，后金(清)的皇帝、后妃们一直生活在这里。

1644年(清顺治元年)，清朝迁都北京，沈阳城尊为陪京(或称留都)，这里的宫殿也就成了"陪京宫殿"只是由皇家派人管理、保护，而不是皇帝、后妃们的经常住所。但是，清朝在全中国的统治基本稳定以后，从康熙皇帝起，始有东巡拜谒祖陵之制。因所祭的福陵、昭陵都在沈阳附近，所以沈阳故宫又成了皇帝东巡时必到的地方。1743年(乾隆八年)，清高宗弘历继位后初次东巡谒陵，来到沈阳故宫，觉得这里应该增建一些供东巡时皇帝后妃使用的宫殿。于是，乾隆十一年至十三年(1746年——1748年)，又在原有中路宫殿之侧兴建了行宫，我们现在称之为"东所"，包括有颐和殿、介祉宫和敬典阁几座建筑。乾隆十九年(1754年)和道光九年(1829年)，弘历(乾隆帝)的母亲和旻宁(道光帝)的母亲随同东巡时就曾住在这里。崇政殿西侧新建的行宫称为"西所"，是供皇帝东巡驻跸使用的。它包括供皇帝东巡时办理政事的迪光殿，皇帝的书房和寝宫——保极宫。行宫建成后，乾隆、嘉庆、道光三位皇帝先后六次东巡时都曾在这里居住。保极宫之后是随驾东巡后妃居住的继思斋。再北是与东所敬典阁遥相对应的同式建筑崇谟阁。这些新盖造的宫殿与当时关内同类建筑的布

局形式和建筑风格相同，而不象入关前的宫殿那样具有浓郁的地方民族特色。只是屋顶采用黄琉璃瓦绿剪边的装饰形式尚与原有宫殿相一致。除东、西所外，这次增建的还有凤凰楼前崇政殿后东西两侧的协中斋、师善斋、日华楼、霞绮楼，以及复建的飞龙阁和翔凤阁等，都是用来贮存宫中物品的库房。

乾隆四十三年(1778年)，弘历第三次东巡来沈阳，又命将原在沈阳大东门外的盛京太庙迁到大清门东侧重建，有正殿三间，东、西配殿各三间，东、西耳房各三间，在大内宫阙东南隅二米多高的土台上形成一座独立的院落。乾隆三十七年起(1772年)，皇帝下令在全国范围内搜集图书，编辑大型的丛书《钦定四库全书》。按照皇帝的旨意，这本书修成后要抄成七份，其中有一份要送到沈阳故宫尊藏。同时还决定，收藏《四库全书》的书阁都要仿照著名的浙江宁波的大藏书家范

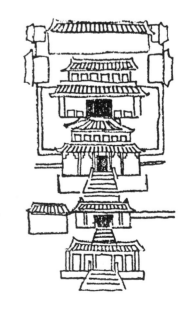

111

钦所建的藏书楼"天一阁"的样式盖造。这样，自乾隆四十六年到四十七年（1781——1782年）又在沈阳故宫的西路兴建以藏书阁——文溯阁为中心的一组建筑，我们现在称其为后期建筑。它大致可分为前、后两部分：南面是以戏台为中心的一组建筑，包括戏台后的扮戏房，戏台前皇帝赏戏的嘉荫堂和两侧供随同官员看戏的宽敞游廊。这些是为皇帝驻跸沈阳故宫期间设宴赏戏而修建的。嘉荫堂之北，便是以文溯阁为中心的一组建筑。文溯阁是一座外观二层，室内三层的楼阁。面阔五间，加上西侧的楼梯间共六间。房顶用黑色琉璃瓦，前后廊彩画及檐柱均以兰、绿等色为主调，与其它宫殿相比显得清新典雅。阁东为一座方形碑亭，内有根据乾隆皇帝亲自撰文刻成的"文溯阁记"石碑。文溯阁后还有仰熙斋，九间殿等建筑，是供皇帝读书、休息时使用的。

文溯阁等宫殿建成后，构成了沈阳故宫西路。这样便形成了东、中、西三路并立的建筑布局和早、中、晚三期共存的积累式面貌。共有各种建筑三百余间，占地面积达六万多平方米，这就是现存的沈阳故宫。

自十九世纪始，清朝的封建统治逐步走向衰落。1829年旻宁东巡之后，就再没有皇帝到沈阳祭祖谒陵，沈阳故宫又被闲置起来，由于这里的宫殿建筑保存的比较完整，宫廷文物也十分丰富，到了清末宣统年间地方的一些官员便向朝廷建议，在文溯阁前的空地上建造一座"皇室博物馆"，把宫殿里所藏珍奇精美的宫廷文物移到那里公开陈列，供中外游人参观。当时的中国人受西方国家的影响，兴办博物馆作为实行社会教育的一项新措施，被加以提倡和实施。但是还没有一座以皇室文物为展品的博物馆。因此，中外人

士听说要在沈阳故宫筹建，都十分欢迎。但是，那时的清政府已经是朝不保夕，根本无意去考虑办什么博物馆。因此没有同意这个建议，不久，清朝的统治便被推翻了。

中华民国成立的初年，沈阳故宫的建筑还作为"皇室产业"，由退位的清朝皇帝派人掌管。1926年冬，当时的奉天省政府将沈阳故宫辟为博物馆。称为"东三省博物馆"。它的宗旨是利用沈阳故宫这处古建筑遗址，发扬地方文明，实施社会教育，促进文化发展。这座博物馆于次年11月16日正式开始办公，第一任馆长曾任国会议员。

1928年冬，奉天省政府将"东三省博物馆"进行改组。组成了以省教育厅厅长和沈阳市市长等人组成的新的博物馆筹备委员会，并决定馆内设古物部和图书部两个业务部门，又特别聘请了清末负责管理故宫的满族

著名文人金梁为筹备委员会委员长。从清理沈阳故宫旧藏宫廷文物入手，拣选陈列物品，以尽快实现为公众开放，由于金梁对沈阳故宫的藏品情况比较熟悉，又具备相应的文物鉴选能力，所以筹备工作进展很快。近四个月时间就挑选出可供陈列的文物数百件，并分别置于各展室中。1929年4月，东三省博物馆共有七个陈列室，都是利用沈阳故宫的宫殿开辟的，很多陈列品都与所在宫殿有着密切的联系，可增加观众的有关知识和参观兴趣，也形成了这座建于沈阳故宫的博物馆应有的特色。使这座昔日的帝王宫殿成为对民众实施社会教育的一个组成部分。成为中国较早开办的博物馆之一。

在此后的两年多里，"东三省博物馆"又有了新的发展。在业务方面，对原有的陈列展览进行了调整和充实。又陆续增辟了宫廷瓷器、殿版图书等几个新陈列室，并将各项展品的说明文字汇辑成册，向观众发售。以使陈列展览收到更好的效果。同时，又通过向社会征集，接受捐献和参加考古发掘等途径增加了一些沈阳地方的历史文物，扩大了收藏和展览品的范围，为了提高业务水平，还着手创办文物博物馆学方面的研究刊物，扩大了在社会上的影响。在管理方面，结合馆务改组制订了《东三省博物馆简章》和古物、图书的收集、保存、阅览办法，展览规则，人员办事细则等一系列规章制度，使各项馆务逐步走上了正常发展的轨道。

1931年9月18日，日本发动了侵略东北的"九一八"事变。沈阳沦陷，"东三省博物馆"也被迫关闭。1932年6月，这座博物馆被改称为"奉天故宫博物馆"恢复开放，共有十一个陈列室，基本仍为东三省博物馆后期的规模。1935年6月，伪"满洲帝国"于沈阳

112

设立"国立博物馆"（后改称国立博物馆奉天分馆）。次年 1 月，便将奉天故宫博物馆关闭，该馆有关历史、艺术的许多藏品，被移往"国立博物馆"，而沈阳故宫则归伪"奉天陵庙承办事务处"管理，使这里又成了不准擅入的禁地。日本投降后，1946年春，国民党政府接收沈阳，在故宫内设立了"辽宁省立民众教育院"，利用遗存的一些文物，在部分宫殿中举办陈列。1947年1月，中央教育部决定，将"国立沈阳博物馆"和"国立沈阳图书馆"合并，以沈阳故宫为遗址组建"国立沈阳博物院"任命著名学者金毓黻为主任委员。准备将该院建成与设在南京的"国立中央博物院""北京故宫博物院"并存的三座大型国立博物院。

中华人民共和国成立后，人民政府在沈阳故宫设立了故宫陈列所。1955年，又在这里设立了清代历史艺术性质的博物馆——沈阳故宫博物馆。国家和地方政府拨出大量资金用于古建筑的维修和保护。使清末以来年久失修的古建筑恢复了金顶朱垣雕梁画栋的昔日风采。1961年，经中华人民共和国国务院批准确定沈阳故宫为"全国重点文物保护单位"。1986年，这座博物馆的名称改为"沈阳故宫博物院"。同年10月，隆重举行了建院六十周年纪念活动，全国各地的许多博物馆界、清史界学者前来祝贺。在这一年举行的全国文博工作会议上，沈阳故宫博物院又被命名为全国文博系统先进单位，成为在国内外有较高知名度的博物馆。1985年至1987年，沈阳故宫中从未对外开放过的嘉荫堂、戏台、文溯阁、继思斋、盛京太庙以及颐和殿、介祉宫、碾房、磨房等处都按历史原状布置陈列对观众开放。使清代沈阳故宫的各主要宫殿都开辟为博物馆的陈列展览场

所，更充分地发挥出这处古建筑群的教育功能。

近几年来，沈阳故宫博物院在业务队伍建设方面也有了明显的进步。先后充实和组建了研究室、陈列部、保管部、技术部、图书档案馆、古建部、群众工作部等业务部门，现已有高、中、初级业务人员一百多人。近年院内业务人员共撰写、出版专著十余本，发表研究文章上百篇，其数量超过前几十年的总和，保证和促进了博物馆业务水平的提高。

清代的沈阳故宫也是与北京故宫，承德行宫并存的三大皇家文物收藏所之一。从乾隆初年开始，按照皇帝的旨意，随时从北京运送宫廷文物到这里收藏，并供皇帝东巡驻跸期间使用，至乾隆末年，沈阳故宫就已经收藏各种宫廷文物十万余件，分别存放于飞

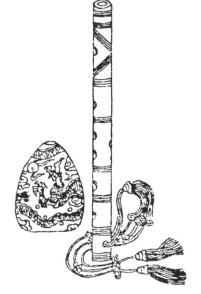

龙阁、翔凤阁、东七间楼等几处库房中，主要有以下几类：

1．古代铜器。共八百件，乾隆四十七年（1782年）由北京运至，包括商、周、汉、唐各代所制鼎、瓿、盂、炉、钟等器，其中很多铜器上还铸有铭文，既是研究当时历史和礼制的实物资料，也是一批珍贵的古代工艺品，后来这些铜器作为清宫藏品的一个重要部分，被专门记入《西清续鉴乙编》一书中。

2．古代书画，包括唐、宋、元、明、清历代书法、绘画作品多幅。其中有闫立本、戴嵩、李公麟、苏轼、蔡襄、朱芾、郭熙、赵孟、钱选、文征明、沈周、仇英、唐寅、董其昌、王原祁、王恽、恽寿平等著名书画家的作品。民国初年金梁据其编辑《盛京故宫书画录》一书，对这些书画逐件作以详细记录。

3．陶瓷器，共10万余件，绝大部分存放在东七间楼"瓷器库"中。基本上都是明清两代江西景德镇官窑制品，有盘、碗、盅、壶、花瓶、笔筒等器物，其中大部分是清代康熙、雍正、乾隆时期生产的，而这一时期正是清代制瓷业发展的高峰。这批瓷器中有青花、五彩、斗彩、法琅彩、霁红、霁青等各种釉色，还有一些仿古代名窑的制品，因为是供皇帝行宫陈设之用，所以具有很高的工艺水平。

4．御用武备，即清代皇帝使用过的刀、矛、弓箭等各类兵器以及马鞍、甲胄等，共有数千件。满族是一个擅长骑射的民族，清代的皇帝也都是从少年时代就开始学习骑马射箭，并且经常外出行围狩猎，他们所使用的一些兵器，被专程送到沈阳故宫"供奉"，以表示不忘祖先传统之意。

5．用于各宫殿陈设的工艺品，有金器、

银器、玉器、珐琅器、漆器、以及犀角、象牙、竹、木等雕刻的工艺品，共有1000多件。其中很多制品不但质料贵重而且造型生动，工艺精美，是清代宫廷中能工巧匠的杰作。

除上述者外，清代沈阳故宫还收藏着许多御用丝织品，各省及全国的舆地图、清代皇帝御制的书画作品等，这些宫廷文物大部分都在民国初年被运往北京收藏于北京故宫博物院，南京博物员，台北故宫博物院等处。未被外运的一部分现为沈阳故宫博物院收藏品。清代沈阳故宫的另一部分珍藏，是清内府写本和刻本书籍，档案，分贮于文溯阁、崇谟阁、敬典阁和四七间楼中。

1. 文溯阁《四库全书》，这是清代乾隆年间纂修的一部大型丛书，分经、史、子、集四部，共收先秦至清代各种书籍3,503种，历时10年始成。当时一共抄写了7部，分别存放在北京、沈阳、承德、杭州、扬州、镇江的七座皇家藏书楼中，沈阳故宫文溯阁所藏《四库全书》共6.144函.36.000多册，分别盛以特制的楠木书匣，摆放在阁内100多个专用书架上，每本书都用绢作封面，纸墨精良，字体娟秀，装帧考究，堪称为一件艺术品，这部《四库全书》至今仍保存完好，成为中国的文化瑰宝。

2. 《清实录》，是清代官修的编年体史书。每代皇帝继位后都要宫中所藏档案修纂前一朝的《实录》，记载其间国家发生的重要事件和皇帝的言行，时称"秘史"。与《实录》同时修纂的还有根据皇帝诏谕分类辑录而成的《圣训》。《实录》、《圣训》修成后各抄写五份，其中四份分存于北京的皇宫，内阁和国家档案库——皇史，另一份由皇帝指派官员专程送到沈阳故宫崇谟阁内收藏至清朝末年始沈阳故宫共储清太祖至穆宗10朝满、汉文《实

录》、《圣训》1.800多包，近一万册。

3. 《满文老档》这是清朝最早的官修史书，它记载了明万历三十五年(1607年)至清崇德元年(1636年)满族兴起，建国直至皇太极改国号为"大清"这一时期的历史，更为珍贵的是它全部用老满文(无圈点满文)写成。此书修成于清太宗时期，清入关后携至北京，乾隆年间为便于保存又用新、老满文字体各抄成两部，分藏北京和沈阳两处皇宫中，民国初年，沈阳故宫崇谟阁所藏的一部首先被发现并逐渐公诸于世，成为国内外学者研究清入关前历史和满族历史，语言最有价值的资料。

4. 《玉牒》即清代爱新觉罗皇家的族谱。按制每隔十年增修一次，"宗室"谱用黄色封面，"觉罗"谱用红色封面，修成后抄为3份，两份留在北京，一份送往沈阳故宫敬典阁存贮，至光绪年间，沈阳故宫共有《玉牒》387包。

此外，沈阳故宫还收藏有《满洲实录》、《汉文旧档》和几万件盛京内务府的满汉文档案。另有乾隆至光绪年间陆续由北京送至沈阳故宫的清内府武英殿刊本书籍，计400多种1.000多部，10.000余册。

现在的沈阳故宫博物院，收藏着以明清历史文物和工艺品为主的数量众多的藏品。有书画、陶瓷器、漆器、珐琅器、玉器、金银器、铜器、碑刻、织绣品，木器家具、珠宝首饰等类其中有清入关前使用的满、蒙文信牌、印牌；清代皇帝使用的弓箭、腰刀、马鞍，康熙、乾隆时期所制用于宫廷典礼的乐器；清宁宫萨满祀用具；盛京太庙收藏的清历朝帝后玉册，玉宝；清太宗皇太极御用鹿角椅；铸有后金天命年号的云版；沈阳太平寺锡伯族家庙满文石碑等，都是珍贵的历

史文物。本院所藏工艺品中大部分是清代宫廷中所用，具有较高的艺术价值。目前，沈阳故宫博物院利用丰富的藏品和保存完好的古代宫殿建筑，开设了20多个陈列室。其中大政殿、崇政殿、清宁宫、文溯阁、东、西(继思斋)驻跸所等都按照历史面貌布置原状陈列。清代兵器、乐器、陶瓷器、漆器、珐琅器、雕刻工艺品、书法绘画，宫廷陈设品、帝后画像等则分别辟以专室展出，并有身着清代服装的女讲解员为观众讲解。每年有二百多万中外游人来这里参观。一九八六年以来，本院文物又先后在加拿大、美国等国展出，受到国外观众的赞赏。

这次应新加坡共和国邀请，沈阳故宫博物院以《清代宫廷历史文物》赴新加坡展出。展览以三百多件，珍贵文物，展出了清初沈阳故宫帝后的生活面貌，包括正殿、寝宫起居、巡幸、狩猎、服饰、宫廷陈设及日常用品。我们相信，通过这次展出会加深新加坡人民对中国历史和文化的了解并进一步增进中新两国人民的友谊。

中国沈阳故宫博物院

114

# 盛京大内的一座独特建筑——继思斋

继思斋，建于清乾隆十一至十三年（1746——1748）是盛京皇宫内一座独具特色的宫室建筑。它坐落在皇宫中路的西所之内，前与迪光殿、保极宫相连，泼以崇谟阁为依，是一处安谧幽静的院落，又是乾隆、嘉庆等皇帝东巡盛京时，妃嫔的寝所。

继思斋是勾连搭三卷棚式屋顶，就是三个卷棚勾连为一个整体的屋顶。进深、面阔均为三间，整体呈正方形，建筑独特。斋内的装修更为精巧别致，均用碧纱隔扇将斋内分成大小相等的九个小间，即相间隔，又至连通，颇有"迷宫"之趣。

这九个小房间，陈设不一，用途各异。正中两个明间相通中间设坐床，其陈设亦如便殿，所以是召见臣仆或嫔妃谒见皇帝的地方。宫灯高悬，晚间照明亦如白昼。一进东西稍间各有圆门锦帐，清静幽雅，为休息的地方，二进西间为佛堂与明间相连，清朝宫中设佛堂的历史由来已久，且极普遍，因为清朝皇帝除视萨满教为第一尊崇的宗教之外。其次就是佛教了。在北京的紫禁城内，就有许多大大小小的殿阁作为佛堂，以便宫中皇帝，后妃顶礼谟拜，如：慈宁宫、寿安宫、佛日楼、养心殿……等内，都设有大小不一的佛堂，所以继思斋里也设有一处小小的佛堂，是专供东巡盛京来的皇帝，妃嫔们在这里向佛祖谟拜的;二进东间与一进东间、明间均以碧纱隔扇门相连，是一处书房、皇帝、妃嫔们皆可悠闲自得的在这里读书写字，或批阅奏章。由此往里走过同样的碧纱隔扇门便进入三进东间，这里透出一股脂粉气，是妃嫔的梳妆间，在雕龙的脸盆架上，端放着錾有花纹的银盆，古香古色的梳妆台，加上玲珑透剔的牙雕首饰盒及一应化妆用品，都显示出这里曾居住过一位端庄、秀美的女主人，她谙扫蛾眉、轻点朱唇、无论早妆、晚妆都要在这里描画。从梳妆室向左，进入三进中间，如入兰室，是她的寝居之所，幔帐低垂、锦衾拥馨，悠悠而传，当然也是皇帝归幸之所。净房与寝宫相连，设在三进的西间里，所谓"净房"，就是"御厕"，内设净器，"净"即是"便盆"。多是用银或银锡合金制成。净要放在净橙之下，相当于今天的坐便，净橙又有"凉净""暖净"之分，顾名思义，凉净为暑日之用，暖净则为温、寒时用。这里的设备可谓应有尽有。

继思斋在大内的诸多宫室中最具有代表性，正应俗语，"麻雀虽小，五脏俱全"之句。这里是清朝宫廷中帝后生活的一个缩影。我们为了使新加坡的观众能更多地了解清代帝后的宫中生活。特把这个斋室按原状复制在这里展出，以飨观者。

中国沈阳故宫博物院

115

# 皇权的象征
## ——大政殿与卤簿仪仗

在中国潘阳故宫博物院赴新加坡共和国《清代帝后文物精华展》中，有一套非常突出，异常珍贵的文物，即清朝皇帝在重大典礼，朝会才御用的。金漆透雕云龙大宝座和金漆云龙七合大屏风，这套宝座、屏风共雕龙一〇三条，它们大小不一，姿态各异，或穿云出水，或翘首赶珠，或团躯俯视，或首尾相联，雕工精湛、气势宏大，威严壮观，堂皇华贵。在我们国内已属罕见的宫廷文物。陈设在大政殿中。

大政殿是潘阳故宫的金鸾殿，始建于清太祖努尔哈赤迁都潘阳之初，凡重大典礼，都在这里举行。清太宗皇太极继汗位之后，天聪元年(1627年)，第一个元旦就是在这举行了朝贺。据《满文老档》天聪元年丁卯正月初一日条载：“诸贝勒大臣及文武官员五更末集于大衙门(即大政殿)各按旗序排列。黎明、聪明汗率诸贝勒大臣诣堂子拜天，行三跪九叩礼而还。汗御衙门，昇座毕，诸贝勒大臣各按旗序，行三跪九叩头礼……是年除夕元旦以太祖丧撤乐停宴，汗仅受众人叩拜礼。一六四四年，清朝第三代皇帝顺治就在这个殿中授他叔文多尔衮大将军印领清兵入关，定鼎北京之后，盛京宫殿成了陪都宫殿，但这里的文武官员依然定期在这里举行“朝贺”仪式。即按入关前的旧制，在这里举行朝贺仪式。

凡遇逢五常朝之日，城内将军、五部、奉天府、承德县等各衙署的官员亦须集于宫殿之前，象征性地行常朝之礼。因为皇帝并不在此地，所以按京城里常朝时皇帝不御殿之例，称之为“坐班”。

至于潘阳故宫当时的“坐班”情形，《大清通礼》等书中，均有较详细的记述，按其所记，每月逢五之黎明，盛京文武各官身着朝服于大政殿“八旗朝堂(即俗称“八旗亭”、十王亭)”前，排定班位。锒黄、正白、锒白、正兰四旗在东，正黄、正红、锒红、锒兰四旗在西；奉天府堂属官(皆为汉人)在锒兰旗之南。众官员又按品级高低，从一品至九品分为九班。将军一班，副都统、五部侍郎一班，巡察御史、奉天府尹、府丞一班，协领、城守卫一班，五部郎中、佐领、治中、五部员外郎、五品世职一班，五部主事、通判，承德县知县、防御一班，七品世职、司库、经历、骁骑校一班，八品笔帖式、教授一班，九品笔帖式、司狱一班。东位西面，西位东面，皆北上。至时(春、冬季辰正，夏、秋季卯正)众官于各朝堂前按班列坐。由盛京礼部赞礼郎二人分左右自班首绕行，记下各官衔名，然后众官各退。

除上述的“朝贺”以外，每年的三大节即：元旦、冬至、万寿节(皇帝诞辰)及逢有国家其它重大庆典之日、盛京各衙署官员还要按制于大政殿前恭行朝贺之礼。

早在皇太极时期，每逢元旦(农历正月初一日)皇帝都要御大政殿，诸王贝勒大臣齐集殿前庆贺大典。遇万寿节也在此处举行贺礼。如《清太宗实录》崇德二年十月己未条载：“万寿节，上御笃恭殿(即大政殿)内外和硕亲王、多罗郡王、多罗贝勒、固山贝子、三顺王及朝鲜质子文武各官上表称贺。

综上所述可见大政殿在潘阳故宫的重要地位。这次展览除以大政殿的全部陈设参展之外。还有一部分皇帝御用卤簿仪仗，这也是目前我国内少见的文物。

卤簿，本来是中国古代皇帝用以体现地位、尊严而建立起来的一种礼仪制度。滥觞于先秦，成熟于汉晋，发展于隋唐，鼎盛于明清。清初也早有定制，当清太宗皇太极继汗位之初便颁有设立大驾卤簿书及赐内外亲王、郡王、贝勒、贝子、公主、格格仪仗书。清代的卤簿仪仗在规模上较为庞大、复杂，乾隆十三年(1748)曾有一次更定，直至清朝覆亡未变。按制，卤簿仪仗分为大驾卤簿、法驾卤簿、銮驾卤簿和骑驾卤簿四等，其用途和用器亦不相同。

皇帝大驾卤簿其使用为皇帝祭圜立、祈谷、常云时、陈大驾卤簿，大阅时诣行宫及礼成还宫时亦用之。

其使用仗器及排列顺序为前列守众四、次列宝象四、次静鞭四、次前部大乐(乐器为大铜角四、小铜角四、金口角四)。次革辂驾马四、木骆驾马六，象辂驾马八，金辂驾象一，玉辂驾象一；次铙歌乐(金二、铜鼓四、铜钹二、扁鼓二、铜点二、龙篴二、平篴二、云锣二、管二、笙二、金口角八、六铜角十六、小铜角十六、蒙古角二、金钲四、角二十四、龙鼓二十四、龙篴十二、相板四、仗鼓四、金四、龙鼓二十四、间以红灯六)。次引仗六、御仗十六、吾仗十六、立瓜、卧瓜各十六、星钺各十六、出警旗一、入跸旗一、五色金龙小旗四十，次翠华旗二、金鼓旗二、门旗八、日、月旗各一、五云旗五、五雷旗五、八风旗八、甘雨旗四、列宿旗四、神武、朱雀、青龙、白虎旗各一、天马、天鹿、辟邪、犀牛、赤熊、黄熊、白泽、冉端、游鳞、红狮、振鹭、鸣鸢、赤鸟、华虫、黄鹄、白雉、云鹤、孔雀、仪凤、翔鸾旗各一。五色龙纛四十、前锋纛人、护年纛人、骁骑纛二十四。次黄麾四、仪铨氅四、黄节四、进善纳言、敷文振武、褒功怀远、行功施惠、明刑弼教、教孝表节旌各二。龙头幡四、豹尾幡四、绛引幡四、信幡四、羽葆幢四、霓幢四、紫幢四、长寿幢四次鸾凤

赤方扇八，单龙黄团扇人，双龙赤团扇八，双龙黄团扇八，赤满单龙团扇六，黄满双龙团扇六，寿字黄扇八。次赤素方伞八，紫素方伞四，五色花伞十，五色妆缎伞十，间以五色九龙团伞十次九龙黄盖二十，紫兰盖二，翠华盖二，九龙曲柄黄盖四。次戟四，殳四，豹尾枪三十，弓矢三十，仪刀三十。次仗马十。次金矛几一，金交椅一，金并二，金盥盘一，金盂一，金盒二，金炉二，拂二。次九龙曲柄黄盖一。前引佩刀大臣十人，提炉二，玉辇在中。后扈佩刀大臣二人，豹尾班执铳佩仪刀侍卫各十人，佩引矢侍卫二十人，领侍卫内大臣一人，侍卫领班二人。后管宗人府王、公二人，散秩大臣一人，前锋护年统领一人，给事中、御史二人，各部郎中、员外郎四人，侍卫班领一人，署侍卫班领一人，侍卫什长二人。次黄龙大纛二，领侍卫内大臣一人，司纛侍卫什长二人，建纛亲笔四人，鸣佩螺亲笔六人。共九百四十九人。真是一个庞大的仪仗队伍，这里展出的就是大驾卤簿中的一部分。

以上卤簿皆为皇帝专设，以示其至高尊贵于万民之上。所以说它也是皇权的一种象征。

中国沈阳故宫博物院

# *Emperors of the Qing Dynasty*

| NAME | YEAR OF BIRTH | YEARS OF REIGN | AGE AT CORONATION |
|---|---|---|---|
| Nurhaci | 1559 | 1616 — 1626 | 58 |
| Huang Tai Ji | 1592 | 1626 — 1643 | 35 |
| Shun Zhi | 1638 | 1644 — 1661 | 6 |
| Kang Xi | 1654 | 1662 — 1722 | 8 |
| Yong Zhen | 1678 | 1723 — 1735 | 45 |
| Qian Long | 1711 | 1736 — 1795 | 25 |
| Jia Qing | 1760 | 1796 — 1820 | 37 |
| Dao Guang | 1782 | 1821 — 1850 | 39 |
| Xian Feng | 1831 | 1851 — 1861 | 20 |
| Tong Zhi | 1856 | 1862 — 1874 | 6 |
| Guang Xu | 1871 | 1875 — 1908 | 4 |
| Xuan Tong (Pu Yi) | 1906 | 1909 — 1911 | 3 |

# Bibliography

*Captions in this book are based on material supplied by the Shenyang Palace Museum.*

*The chapters on Shenyang Palace, Pageantry and Ceremony and The Pavilion of Continuing Thought are based on essays provided by The Shenyang Palace Museum. The articles, in Chinese, are reproduced in Appendix I.*

Gai Ruizhong. *Chinese Art and Craft* (in Chinese). Lion Cultural Press. 1977.

Hook, Brian, gen ed. *The Cambridge Encyclopedia of China*. Cambridge University Press. 1982.

Jiang Xiangshun, Tong Yue. *The Imperial Palace at Shenyang* (in Chinese). Shenyang Publishing House. Shenyang. 1987.

Jingdezhen Porcelain Research Centre. *Chinese Porcelain* (in Chinese). Zong Hua Bookstore, Hong Kong Branch. Hong Kong. 1975.

Li Yu. *A Survey of Chinese Art* (in Chinese). Zong Hua Bookstore, Hong Kong Branch. Hong Kong. 1973.

Shenyang Palace Museum. *Symbols of Imperial Power — The Grand Administration Hall and the Lu Bu Pageants* (in Chinese). pp 116 Imperial Life in the Qing Dynasty. Historical and Cultural Exhibitions Pte Ltd. Singapore. 1989.

Shenyang Palace Museum. *The Pavilion of Continuing Thought — A Unique Palace Building in the Shenyang Palace Complex* (in Chinese). pp 115 Imperial Life in the Qing Dynasty. Historical and Cultural Exhibitions Pte Ltd. Singapore. 1989.

Shenyang Palace Museum Editorial Committee. *Qing Costumes. Exhibition Catalogue* (in Chinese). Shenyang Palace Museum. Shenyang. 1986.

Tie Yuqing, ed. *The Shenyang Palace* (in Chinese). Shenyang Publishing House. 1987.

Tie Yuqing. *Treasures of the Shenyang Palace Museum* (in Chinese). pp 110 Imperial Life in the Qing Dynasty. Historical and Cultural Exhibitions Pte Ltd. Singapore. 1989.

Tie Yuqing, Shen Changji. *Shenyang Palace* (in Chinese). Liao Yu Pubishing House. Shenyang. 1895.

Wan Yi, Wang Shuqing, Lu Yanzhen. *Qing Imperial Life* (in Chinese). The Commercial Press Ltd. Hong Kong. 1985.

Wang Shuqing, Li Pengnian. *Life in the Qing Palaces* (in Chinese). Senyang Palace Publishing House. Shenyang. 1986.

Wang Yunying. *Manchu Costumes of the Qing Period* (in Chinese). Liao Yu Publishing House. Shenyang. 1985.

Yap, Yong & Cotterell, Arthur. *Chinese Civilization: From Ming Revival to Chairman Mao*. Weidenfeld & Nicolson. 1977.